Autism Goes to School

Book One of the School Daze Series

Dr. Sharon A. Mitchell

Other Books in the Series:

Autism Goes to School

Autism Runs Away

Autism Belongs

Autism Talks and Talks

Autism Grows Up

Autism Boxed Set - Help for Home & School

Autism Goes to School Workbook (coming in2017)

Prequel to Autism Goes to School (coming in 2017)

DEDICATION

To Derek

Who always thinks it can be done

This book is proud to be a B.R.A.G. Bronze Medallion Honoree

Contents

ACKNOWLEDGMENTS

To all those with autism, their families and teachers from
whom we learn so much.

CHAPTER 1

Ben grabbed for Kyle's hand as they approached the front of the school. As usual, Kyle cringed and pulled away.

"All right, all right, just come on already. We're late. You have to get to school." I hate being late, Ben muttered to himself. He pulled on the door handle. Nothing. He heaved. "Shit!" Nothing. Kyle, who had remained silent for the last half hour, repeated, "Shit! Shit, shit, shit, shit, shit."

"No. You can't say that." Ben so badly wanted his son to talk to him, but did the kid have to repeat the one taboo word Ben had uttered so far today? He searched for another door, spotted one farther down the building and again reached for Kyle's hand. The sound Kyle let out made him drop it. "Kyle, come on," Ben told his son, "we have to get in there." Kyle came, but, "Shit, shit, shit" came faintly from his mouth. Ben sighed.

It took three doors and more expletives before Ben found one that would allow them to enter the building. He had no idea what was wrong with this place. A school was a public building, wasn't it?

Once in the school, Ben stopped. He had not thought this far. Did he have to find the room for five year olds on his own? He spotted a sign telling visitors to report to the office and an arrow pointing down the beige hall. Without thinking, Ben put his hand on Kyle's shoulder to steer him in the right direction. Predictably, Kyle pulled away, rubbing the shoulder that Ben had touched. Ben winced. "Well, just come then, if you don't want me touching you." Whatever Kyle might be thinking didn't register on his face, but he followed Ben anyway.

In the distance, screaming started up. Ben instinctively stepped in front of his son. He stopped. Where was that coming from? Was a child in danger? What kind of a school was this anyway?

They continued cautiously, Ben ready to grab Kyle and run. The screams became louder as they came to an open door. Inside Ben glimpsed some kids sitting around tables, one in a rocking chair, others standing in front of easels and one little boy writhing on the floor as a woman knelt beside him, about to lay a blanket over him. What the hell were they doing to that child to cause him to scream like that?

Ben glanced at Kyle to make sure he was safe, then stepped into the doorway, ready to intervene. As he watched, the woman spoke softly to the screaming child and laid the blanket over him. She pressed it down firmly around him but the blanket didn't mold to the child's body the way a blanket should. As she continued to press down with the blanket, the screams lessened to whimpers. The woman then reached for a large plastic ball and started running it up and down the little boy's body, pressing harder than Ben would have thought advisable. This was a small child, after all.

"Hey," Ben called. "What are you doing to that kid? Is he all right?" All eyes turned to him. The wailing momentarily eased then started up again. With a nod to a younger woman, the teacher or whoever she was rose to her feet, keeping pressure on the ball until the other woman came to take her place. Then her calm expression changed as she came toward Ben with purpose.

"Please leave my room. You're disturbing my students," she said when she got to the doorway where Ben stood.

Ben looked at her. "I'm disturbing your students?" he asked incredulously. "It looks like you're torturing that poor kid." The kid in question, calm now, looked out at him with big eyes.

"Does he look disturbed?" the teacher asked. "Don't answer that," she added. "This is my classroom and these are my students. Kindly carry on with your own business. If you're new here, the office is that way." She pointed in the direction Ben and Kyle had been going.

"I don't know what your problem is, lady, but I heard a kid screaming and thought he might need help." Ben backed out the door, shaking his head. His heart settled back into its normal pattern after the fright of hearing the child's screams. He'd never let anyone like that near his son.

The office resembled a jungle with green plants everywhere. They were greeted by a welcoming, grey-haired woman, half-hidden by the counter. She stuck out her hand. "Good morning, you two. I'm Mrs. Billings."

Ben shook her hand. "Ben Wickens and this is my son, Kyle". Kyle neither looked at them, nor showed any sign he noticed the smile and hand extended his way. "Ah, Kyle's a little stand-offish at first," he explained.

"Well, I'm sure we'll become firm friends in no time. How may I help you?"

"Kyle is new to the area and needs to be in school."

"Let me introduce you to Dr. Hitkins, our principal. She'll get you registered and in the right classroom."

Ben sank into the chair, fidgeting and expecting a long wait. Bureaucrats did that sort of thing, of course. They'd show him how important they were by keeping him waiting. He hated it, but he'd suffer through it for the sake of his son.

Pulling back his sleeve cuff to check his watch, Ben then glanced at Kyle. Shirt was clean; pants looked all right. He'd

3

remembered to rub the milk off Kyle's mouth. Yep, he looked pretty typical.

The realization hit him once again that yes, he indeed did have a son. The kid was actually quite cute, even if he was biased. Kyle stood at the side of the room, his little body swaying in rhythm to the asparagus fern blowing in the breeze coming through the open window. Ironic. Of all the houseplants in the world, this was one of the very few Ben could actually name. And, this was one his son obviously was attracted to. As he watched, he noticed his son's lips moving, keeping time to the swaying. What was he saying? Ben got up and moved closer.

"Shit, shit, shit, shit," Kyle said. Quietly, at least, thank god.

"Kyle. Shhhh. Don't say that. It's not a nice word." Kyle turned to look at his dad. His eyes actually met Ben's momentarily, before sliding away. Whoa. When was the last time Kyle had looked at him, even briefly?

"Kyle, that's a bad word. Daddy should not have said that. I was frustrated, is all. No, that's not an excuse. I'm sorry you heard that, but please don't say that word."

"Shit, shit, shit, shit," Kyle intoned.

Ben was about to try again when the inner door opened and a middle-aged woman came out smiling, with her hand ready to take Ben's.

"Hi. I'm Dr. Delora Hitkin, principal of Madson Elementary School. What can I do for you?"

Ben introduced himself as he shook her hand. He then pointed to Kyle. "This is my son, Kyle. He needs to start school, but at the moment he seems fascinated by your plants."

"He's not the only one. I love them as well." She turned to Kyle. "Hi, Kyle. Welcome to our school."

Ben started to apologize for his son's behavior. Kyle was so intent on the swaying plant that he did not seem to even notice the principal's presence. Dr. Hitkin waved her hand at Ben's consternation. "Don't worry. We're used to kids here and all are welcome."

She went to the plant and ducked underneath it. She swayed her head in time with the plant, smiling at Kyle. Ben held his breath, waiting for Kyle to explode.

Kyle froze. Ben stepped forward to interfere but Marie, the secretary gave him a warning look.

Kyle's gaze shifted from the plant to the person who dared interfere with his pleasure. Eventually, he met Dr. Hitkin's eyes. She grinned and said, "Boo!"

Ben was amazed and relieved to hear Kyle's giggle. Phew! A crisis averted. He so didn't want Kyle to create a scene even before he'd been accepted into the school.

This brought Ben back to the dilemma that kept him up all night. Should he pass Kyle off as just a typical five year old? Or did he let the cat out of the bag and admit that Kyle had autism? If he told them, what if they would not let Kyle enter the school? What if there was a special school just for morons or kids who had things like autism? What if they didn't want Kyle?

"Mr. Wickens, would you like to come into my office with me?" Ben hesitated. Dr. Hitkin continued, "Kyle will be just fine here with Ms. Billings. She's a great fan of all kids and they adore her." What could Ben say? Should he tell her that Kyle's not like other kids? Before he could decide, Dr. Hitkin ushered him into her office. His last glimpse of Kyle was of Ms. Billings dragging out a tub of chunky, wooden building blocks and getting onto the floor beside Kyle.

"Don't worry, they'll be fine," Dr. Hitkin assured him. "We'll leave the door open so he can see you."

"Now, we have some paperwork to fill out. Will your wife be joining us?"

Ben thought he'd stepped into it already. How to explain the situation without making either he or Deanna sound like a horse's ass?

"No. I'm a single parent. "The words sounded strange to his ears. "Kyle lives with me."

"School started two weeks ago. Why didn't you register him earlier?"

There was no easy way to get around this. He didn't want this new school to be prejudiced against Kyle because of his wacky parents.

"Kyle has only been living with me since yesterday. Prior to that he was with his mother and her husband in California. I now have custody."

"I see. I'll need to retain a copy of the legal custody agreement for the school records."

Ben stared at her. He had no such thing. Damn Deanna. Why had she not mentioned these details? Kyle had been in school before, so surely she must have known.

"Ah, that is still in the works. His mother just sent him to me yesterday and in the rush of exchanging information and Kyle's things, we didn't get to the legal parts. I'll contact her today and get this straightened out. I'm sure there will be no problem."

"Are there any other problems you want to tell me about?"

Ben tried not to squirm. "What do you mean?"

"Let me get one thing straight." Ben's heart filled with dread. Dr. Hitkin had sensed something different about Kyle and was going to say he didn't belong in this school. She continued, "Madson Elementary is a public school. Here we welcome all students. We respect the different learning styles of all children. Do you have any questions or concerns?"

This was obviously the opening for Ben to talk about Kyle's autism. But, he didn't know how to do that, hardly had any idea what autism was all about, other than the quick website search he'd done after Kyle went to bed yesterday. What he read left his mind boggling. The stories! Surely, they did not fit Kyle. Ben didn't know if he could cope, but he sure could not function if Kyle was not in school all day. He had a business to run.

A good defense is a good offence in the business world, Ben believed, so he launched in. "I have certain requirements for my son. I want him in a safe environment. I want him to learn. I want him to have good role models."

Dr. Hitkin nodded.

"I do have some concerns," Ben launched in. "First, you said that this is a public school. As such, I would think that it's a public building. I'll have you know that I had to try three doors before I could find one that let us in. What if there was a fire? How would all these children get out?"

Again, Dr. Hitkin nodded. "And did you notice which one opened for you?" She didn't wait for his reply. "The main door, the one that leads directly to the office. We keep all other doors locked during the day. The one you used is monitored by camera at all times. When the door opens, we're alerted in the office and Marie or I watch the monitor. This is for the safety of our students. We need to know at all times who is in our building and if anyone leaves. And, for your information, in case of a fire alarm, all the other doors are automatically unlocked. Does that answer your question?"

Ben was a little ashamed, but had more. "As we walked along the hall, we came across this one room, not the kind of place I would like any child of mine."

"What exactly do you mean?"

"This little boy was screaming. He was just a small child. A woman, I presume his teacher, threw this big blanket over him and held it down. Then she took this huge ball and put in on top of him. I could see the muscles in her arms working as she pressed down on it!"

"And, what did the child do?" Dr. Hitkin inquired.

"Ah, well, he got quieter, or at least he seemed to."

"And what about the rest of the children in the room?"

"What do you mean?" Ben asked.

Dr. Hitkin clarified. "What were they doing while this was taking place?"

"I didn't pay a lot of attention to them; my concern was all for that one boy," said Ben.

"Think back. Did they look sad? Distressed? Unhappy? Shocked?"

"I don't know them well enough to say, but no, come to think about it, they seemed to be carrying on their business."

"Could you describe the teacher to me?" Dr. Hitkin asked.

Ben gave a brief description of the teacher and the room's location.

"That is Ms. Nicols room. Melanie Nicols is a stellar kindergarten teacher, one of the best you will ever come across."

"I'd have to object to her methods or at least those I witnessed." Ben thought a minute. "Kindergarten? Isn't that for five year olds? Kyle's five. Is that where you think you're going to place him? Oh, no. That's not the place for my son. He's delicate and impressionable. I don't want him exposed to kids who scream or get thrown to the floor."

"Did you see Ms. Nicols or anyone else throw that boy to the floor?" the principal asked.

"Well, no, but...."

"I can assure you that his teacher did not throw him or any other student to the floor." She watched Kyle and Marie through the open door for a minute. "Mr. Wickens, can you honestly tell me that Kyle has never screamed?"

Ben told her, "Come on. He's a child. No child is perfect."

"Exactly. But there is a range that we normally think of as typical for children of a certain age. Then, there are other children of the same age who may do some of the things just like others their age, but may have some, shall we say, quirks. Do you ever see that in Kyle?"

"He's my son. He's the only five year old I know. I don't really have anything to compare him to."

"Mr. Wickens, I presume that you were once a five year old boy yourself. And surely you've seen children in parks and malls and on television. Can you honestly say that Kyle is just like the everyday, typical little boy?"

Ben bristled. "Are you saying there's something wrong with my son?"

"Not at all. I would never suggest that there is anything wrong about any child. Different, yes. Wrong, no. There's a difference."

Ben sighed. He was new at this parenting thing. This crafty old lady was not going to let things slide by. As Ben hesitated, he heard a giggle in the outer office. His head whipped around. Yes, it was Kyle! It was his son. He was actually giggling. Ben watched in amazement. He had not known Kyle had it in him. He was pleased at the sound of the childish delight but saddened that it took a stranger to bring out that glee. Kyle would barely even look at his own father, let alone play with him.

His gaze came back to Dr. Hitkin who was watching him intently. "You're new to this, aren't you Mr. Wickens?" she asked.

Ben wanted to squirm like a little boy sent to the principal's office. "Yes, ma'am," he said reflexively. "Kyle just came to live with me yesterday."

She smiled at him. "I don't mean just new to parenting. I meant that you're new to autism, aren't you?"

Ben stared at her. How the hell did she know? Did Kyle have a big "A" stenciled on his forehead? Or did he himself? Could she tell already that he was the kind of father who would create a kid with autism? Would they turn them away if they thought Kyle had autism?

Ben's back was up again. He needed to defend his son. "Kyle's a good kid, really he is. He's just new to me and to Madson. It's normal to have a period of adjustment. He'll be fine.

I'll be fine. I'll support the school and help out and join the PTA or whatever it is you have these days."

Dr. Hitkin grinned. "Good to know. We'll hold you to that."

He blanched; she smiled as if she was enjoying this.

"You're in luck. Kyle has autism and we just happen to have an autism specialist in the building - Ms. Nicols."

"Not that teacher, that woman who held the kid down and pounded on him with a ball? That lady is not getting anywhere near my son. I will not have him treated that way."

"That woman is a highly trained teacher with a Master's degree in autism. She was not, nor would she ever "pound" on a child. What she was doing was calming him down. You heard his screaming as you came in. You witnessed him calm down under the gentle pressure of the weighted blanked and the ball. Many kids with autism react positively to weight and pressure. You ought to try it with Kyle."

"Let's get one thing straight. There is nothing wrong with Kyle. He's just a little boy. He does not talk much but it's coming. Yeah, Deanna said that when he was younger some doctors said he had autism. But we spent thousands of dollars on treatment over the last three years, pretty much a normal person's salary in a year went to just Kyle's ABA treatment. They said it would cure him and that if we did this intensely, he'd be typical by the time he went to school. Well, he's school age now and I want him in school."

"Certainly he should be in school and he is welcome here. In fact, he can either start tomorrow or spend the rest of today with us. He will be in Ms. Nicols room. It's the ideal spot for him. I guarantee you'll be pleased at his progress. Both he and you will learn a lot."

"Me? I finished school a long time ago."

"True, but now that autism has come into your life, there is suddenly a lot more to learn, isn't there? Don't worry. We'll help."

The principal excused herself to get the paperwork started and left Ben alone with his thoughts. Unfortunately. That damn principal had said the word "autism". How did she know? He hadn't mentioned it.

Usually he was pretty good at paperwork. He was, after all an accountant and dealt in papers much of his waking life. But he'd never before registered a little boy in school. What sort of questions might he be asked? He already failed the test about custody papers. What else didn't he know about his son?

Actually, a lot. He thought back to last night, his first night alone with Kyle. His son; he actually had a son.

He remembered the shock when he first learned that he had a child. But back then, it had still been an abstract concept. Sure, he'd stepped up and supported him financially as soon as he learned of his existence, but that was about it. Deanna would not allow him to meet their son, saying it would be too confusing for Kyle. And, to be honest, Ben had not protested too hard. He had his own life, far, far away from where Kyle and Deanna lived in California His conscience told him it was enough to send money. Lots of money, considering the size of the child.

He had not given much thought to what it would have been like to live with Kyle day by day. Sure, Deanna had said that Kyle had autism and therefore needed all this expensive treatment in order to be cured. But what must life have been like for Deanna before treatment if this was the way Kyle was AFTER treatment?

Last night had been hell, just hell and Ben finally fell into bed exhausted. Then, he thought about it from Kyle's point of view. Maybe it had not been so nice for him either.

Kyle was just a small boy. The kid didn't know him from any stranger on the street. He'd never had such a long car ride before.

There'd been the hysterical call from Deanna saying that she couldn't take it anymore. She and her new husband, Neil, were expecting their first baby together. She had morning sickness, was exhausted and just could not cope with Kyle any longer. She had to concentrate on this new life she was creating and on her marriage. Kyle was just too much for her - for them. It was now Ben's turn.

Before Ben could marshal his arguments and tell her how ridiculous this was, Deanna had hung up, sobbing. Ben assumed he'd hear from her next with apologies, saying she hadn't meant it and all their lives would return to normal.

Instead, just after supper last night there was a knock at the door. A car idled at the curb. In front of him stood a woman and a small boy. If Ben hadn't just talked to her on the phone, he would not have recognized Deanna. Her face was drawn and haggard. She'd aged considerably in the short six years since he'd last seen her when she moved to California, after amiably breaking it off with him.

That had been no big shock or heartbreak. While they'd had a good run briefly, their ardor had paled quickly and they remained buddies with separate lives. He'd wished her well and not thought about her again until the phone call three years ago. Again, Deanna had called him sobbing. She'd told him they shared a son. Kyle had been born eight months after she left for California. Ben didn't question if Kyle was his; Deanna had sobbed on.

Kyle was not a normal child, she said. What? He had autism. He spent his days screaming. He'd been just diagnosed and the treatment - THE treatment was ABA, Applied Behavior Analysis, the only proven treatment for autism, or so they told her. He needed this treatment if he even had a hope of being normal. Whatever normal was, Ben thought.

So, get it for him, Ben said. What's the problem? Well, it seemed the problem was money. The treatment did not come cheap. It required forty hours a week of one on one treatment with a trained therapist. The cost was exorbitant.

Ben had paled when he heard the cost. But, this was his son, even if this was the first he had heard of him. An errant thought entered his mind. Was this really his son? How did he know? He pushed that notion away. His son, his responsibility.

For some time now, Ben had been squirreling away money for a down payment for a house. Sure, this condo was handy, right in the same building as his office, but it was more a place to crash than a home. While he didn't imagine picket fences, he still had an image of a house in his future one day.

The money in his house fund would cover about a year and a half of Kyle's fifty thousand a year therapy. He'd worry about the rest later. Then another thought hit him. How had Deanna managed when she was pregnant? Who had looked after her? How had she handled money when she was unable to work?

Deanna admitted to dipping into her savings. She insisted she had been all right. Since it had been her choice to have a child alone, she had not wanted to ask anything of him.

How had this happened, Ben wanted to know. Well, it wasn't quite the accident he'd assumed. The idea of being a mom had blossomed in Deanna's mind. She knew that her relationship with Ben was more friendship than marriage material. She decided to have a child on her own. Ben was a nice guy, good looking and intelligent; he seemed an acceptable sperm donor, a father she could look back on fondly. She'd stopped taking her birth control pills and assured Ben that his condoms were not necessary.

And you didn't think about letting me in on these plans, Ben had asked, his anger rising. He tamped it down. What's done was done and now Kyle was his responsibility. Deanna should have been as well, if only he'd known about the pregnancy. He quickly calculated what it might have cost to feed and clothe a baby. Maybe five hundred dollars a month? Hell, he didn't know. That worked out to six thousand dollars a year and Kyle was now two and a half years old. That meant he owed Deanna fifteen thousand dollars in back child support. She must have had to take time off work as well. He had sent her a check for twenty-five thousand dollars the next morning and began the monthly installments of two thousand for the part of the treatment costs insurance didn't cover, plus another five hundred for Kyle's keep.

His thoughts were interrupted by the return of Dr. Hitkins with her papers.

"Most of this is just basic information like your address and contact numbers in case we need to reach you during the day. Then we need his medical information."

"Medical?" Ben asked. "He's a pretty healthy kid." His voice broke on the word healthy. Was Kyle actually healthy? Is autism a disease? Was he sick? And, apart from the autism, how was his health? Had he had those things kids get like measles and mumps? Ben had no idea about his own son.

"By medical, for now I just mean his doctor's name and contact information."

Well, he wouldn't get parent of the year award yet again. Ben had no clue who Kyle's doctor was or if he'd ever seen a physician. Ben didn't even have the name of a doctor or one of his own he could use to fake it.

There was so much he didn't know about this little man who was his son. Best 'fess up and try to maintain as much dignity as possible. "Kyle has only just moved to town and I have not yet had time to set him up with a local doctor." Nor had he even thought about it, Ben admitted to himself. "I'll get you this information as soon as possible, but Kyle's healthy and I'm sure calling his doctor won't be necessary."

"I see you left the section on custodial care blank. That is required information. In this era of non-traditional families, we need to know who has legal access to the child, who to send reports to and that sort of thing," Dr. Hitkins explained.

"I have full custody, "Ben replied.

"I don't dispute that but I'm sure you'll understand that for our records we require a copy of the legal custodial order."

Damn Deanna for not mentioning this. "I'll get that to you as soon as possible as well. Can Kyle start school without it?"

"Is there any way you can prove that you have custody and the right to enroll this child in school?"

Ben thought a minute. "What if you phoned his mother? Could she confirm consent over the phone?"

"It's not the usual process but for now it could do," Dr. Hitkins said as Ben pulled out his phone to find Deanna's number.

The ensuing conversation between the principal and Deanna was brief. It sounded like Deanna was trying to get off the phone, while Dr. Hitkins attempted to probe for more information and asked for copies of previous reports.

"Well," she said, "his mother certainly does not dispute that she wants you to have full say and responsibility for your son." She looked at Ben compassionately. "I think she will be sending you copies of medical reports and treatment notes. It would be helpful if you'd be willing to share them with us."

"Those are from when Kyle was much younger. He's better now and ready for school." Again, he received that look but this time it almost showed pity.

"Shall we collect Kyle now and proceed to the classroom? I'm sure you'll want to meet the teacher."

CHAPTER 2

As Ben followed Dr. Hitkins out of her office, he stopped to stare at his son. Kyle was no longer playing with the blocks on the floor but was back staring at the swaying plant. He stood on his tip toes and his little body moved in time with the plant. As Ben watched, Kyle's hands rose to his sides. His hands flapped. A sound came out of his mouth but Ben could not make out what it was. What would Dr. Hitkins think of Kyle if she saw him pulling this kind of stunt?

Ben turned to find her watching him, not Kyle. "Um, he's…," Ben tried to explain.

The principal interrupted. "He's just fine." She planted herself directly in front of Kyle, moved the plant aside and told him to come with her and his dad now. They were going to meet his new teacher.

To Ben's surprise and relief, Kyle lowered himself back down to his heels, turned and followed the principal. Ben trailed behind, adding, "Just as long as it's not that room where the kid was screaming. I don't want Kyle upset by seeing things like that going on."

Dr. Hitkins just looked over her shoulder at him and continued down the hall. She stopped before that very doorway and without waiting for Ben, rapped twice on the open door, placed her hands firmly on Kyle's shoulders and moved him into the classroom.

Ben was about to warn her to get her hands off Kyle because he hated to be touched, when he noticed his son standing quietly with the principal's palms firmly on his shoulders. "Kyle, Mr. Wickens, I'd like you both to meet Kyle's new teacher, Ms. Melanie Nicols. Ms. Nicols, I'm pleased to bring you a new student, Kyle and his dad, Mr. Ben Wickens."

That woman, the one who had crushed the little boy under the blanket then squashed him with a ball, approached Kyle with a smile. Her hair was pulled back into a tight, low pony-tail. Her clothing suited her hair, plain and practical. She knelt in front of him and held out her hand. Kyle stared out the window.

"Hi, Kyle," she said. "I'm Ms. Nicols. I'm your teacher. Will you look at me?" She remained perfectly still, waiting. And waited. And waited. Ben grew uncomfortable and started to intervene. One look from Ms. Nicols and he froze. After an eternity, Kyle shifted his gaze from the window to his new teacher. "Hi," she repeated. "In this room you are free to explore. Go ahead and take a look around."

Ben tried to apologize. "Look, he doesn't talk much."

"Oh, really?" Ms. Nicols raised her eyebrow at him.

Ben felt his temper rising. "Yes, really. He's just a little boy who's been uprooted and brought to a new home, a strange city and..." He stopped himself. He'd almost said "and to a strange father". That was too much information.

Ms. Nicols repeated that they were welcome to wander around and explore the classroom. Without even glancing back at Ben, Kyle took off, dragging his hand along the wall of the classroom.

"Kyle. Kyle, come back here," Ben called.

"He's fine, just let him go," Ms. Nicols interrupted him. Kyle ignored his father anyway.

Ben glared at her, not feeling good about relinquishing control of his son to a stranger - to this stranger in particular. Dr. Hitkin motioned to the younger woman who was talking with some children. When she came up to them, Dr. Hitkin said, "Mr. Wickens, I'd also like you to meet Ms. Lori Nabaku. She's the EA in the room." Seeing Ben's perplexed look, she explained, "That stands for Educational Associate. Kyle is lucky; there are two adults in this room rather than just one teacher." She continued, "Lori, this is Mr. Ben Wickens. His son's name is Kyle and he'll be joining your classroom." They all turned to look at Kyle.

As they watched Kyle, a little boy approached the group of adults. He walked close to Ben, stared him up and down, then walked in a circle around him. The circling became faster and the look on the boy's face changed. His breathing hitched, and then he backed away from Ben with a look of terror on his face. He opened his mouth and these awful noises came out. Ben felt as if he was strangling a kitten.

"What? What? I didn't do anything. What's the matter with him?" Ben asked.

"Lose the aftershave," Ms. Nicols told him.

"What"

By this time she had the boy slung across her arms. and was carrying him toward a bean bag couch at the side of the room. The child's eyes never left Ben, and the look of terror remained. Ms. Nicols sat on the bean bag with the child, holding him close. Gradually the child's noises subsided and tears ran down his cheeks. Ms. Nicols got up and returned with a flat, stuffed animal that she placed on the boy's lap. His hands immediately went to the tufts of hair and his fingers pulled at the strands over and over. But, at least he was calm.

Ben looked at the principal. "What just happened here?"

"Some children are extremely sensitive to things like sounds and smells. Daniel there reacts intensely to smells. Your aftershave, as Ms. Nicols pointed out, can seem overpowering to one with such sensitivities. Daniel was curious about you and likely would have struck up a conversation with you once he had determined that you were safe, but then he smelled your cologne and that took over any other thoughts or plans he might have had."

"Jeez. I didn't know. Sorry. Should I go apologize to him or would that set him off again."

"I think it best you not go anywhere near him right now. His system is just starting to calm down. There are reasons that this is a scent-free building. A number of our children have similar sensitivities. Surely you saw the notice when you came in the front door? It's also posted in all the hallways."

"I might have seen it but would not have known what it meant," Ben admitted.

"This is something to keep in mind now that Kyle is living with you. I don't know if it's the case with him but many children with autism spectrum disorders have these sensitivities."

Ben looked at her. "That's the second time you've made reference to the word autism about Kyle. I never said he still has autism. What makes you think that?"

They both turned to look at his son. Kyle was standing with his body angled to the sun streaming through the windows. Dust motes were visible. Kyle had his hands up and his fingers danced through the sun's rays. He was standing on his toes and a delighted smile marked his face. He truly seemed to be enjoying the way his fingers moved through the sun light.

Ben sighed. The principal quirked an eyebrow at him.

"All right. I still have trouble believing this, but when Kyle was two, this team of doctors diagnosed him with autism. They said he was delayed in many areas and didn't speak. But we got him all the treatment they said he needed. They said if he had this early and intensive treatment that he'd be cured and ready for school by age five. We paid for forty hours a week of ABA for three years. Well, he's five now. But look at him!" Ben ran his hand over his face.

"Mr. Wickens, Kyle *IS* ready for school. He's here now and here he shall stay. He'll be fine. He will learn and progress. Autism is not a dirty word. It's a different way of viewing the world. There are challenges involved in autism, for sure. But, there are also strengths."

Ben looked at her. "Right now, I'm not seeing a lot of those strengths."

"You will and we'll help both you and Kyle to learn and appreciate those strengths. The other things we'll work on together." Strange, but Ben felt somewhat reassured by this steady woman.

Now that the crisis seemed over and the teacher rejoined them, Ben apologized. "I'm sorry. I didn't know. I didn't mean to upset anyone.

Ms. Nicols ignored that and asked, "Do you have any questions about our program here?"

"Actually, I do. Just what kind of a place is this? I know that economic times are hard, but can't the school district even afford desks for kids? Or real furniture instead of this mishmash of plastic whatevers?" He gestured to the eclectic seating arrangements in the room. There were rocking chairs – adult and kid sized. While there were a few regular chairs, some of the kids actually had to sit on big plastic balls. They looked more solid than beach balls, sort of like ones he'd seen at his gym. A couple other kids sat on plastic stools that looked like mushrooms but the bottoms were not flat, forcing the children to rock slightly and shift their weight to balance. Then another poor kid was forced to perch on a stool that had only one leg in the middle of it.

"I can assure you, Mr. Wickens, that there is a reason for everything you see in this classroom and for everything we do here."

"I mean, I know this is only kindergarten, but there's not a blackboard in sight. How do you teach kids without a blackboard?"

Ms. Nicols directed his attention to the front of the room where three children were gathered around a white screen on the wall. At first Ben thought it was just a projector screen and said, "Hey, look what he's doing," as he saw a kid pick up a marker and draw on it.

"I take it you're not familiar with interactive white boards, Mr. Wickens?" Then, to the students, "Gracie, Mack, James, please show Kyle's dad how you use that program." The kids proceeded to touch the screen, circle objects, drag objects, then capture the image before moving on to the next page.

"Wow. That ain't your mama's blackboard."

Up to now, the principal had stood watching this interaction with a twinkle in her eye. At Ben's next statement, she stiffened.

"Since you asked if I have questions, yes, I do have more. Why are those kids here?" Ben nodded his head at two children in wheelchairs with half-moon tables pulled over the armrests of their chairs. One kid seemed to be laboring away at some paper task, while another painstakingly moved a game piece around a board as two other students eagerly awaited their turn at the game.

"Just what do you mean?"

"I mean, what kind of a classroom is this? You seem to have all sorts of kids in here."

"Exactly."

"Well, my son's not like that. He doesn't talk much, but he needs good role models and a place to learn." He looked over at Kyle who was still entranced by the dust motes visible in the sunlight streaming through the window. Kyle had his hand up and was watching the sunlight play on his fingers. Ben sighed. The teacher looked at Kyle then at Ben.

"You were saying?" she prompted.

This was not easy and she was not cutting him any slack.

The principal intervened. "Why don't you take a look around the room Mr. Wickens and get a feel for the class."

Ms. Nicols left him. To Ben's amazement, she picked up a book and crawled into a tent at the back of the room. Quickly two students joined her in the tent. Ben could hear her voice reading them a story. Kyle edged closer until he could peek inside. Ms. Nicols invited Kyle to come listen and to Ben's surprise, his son crawled in. Once the story was over, the kids left the tent and went back to their odd seating arrangements. Kyle checked out the displays on the back counter.

Ben watched a little girl swivel in her seat, pick up some metal contraptions, fit her arms through leather straps then heave herself to her feet, relying on the crutches for support. This ungainly walk took her near the back of the room where Kyle was. Ben held his breath, waiting for Kyle to react in fear. The girl flashed Kyle a smile, reached for a bucket of crayons and returned to her table. Kyle showed far less discomfort than Ben.

He tried again with Ms. Nicols. "Look. Kyle is a normal little boy. I'm not sure he belongs here. He's not like these kids."

Just then there was a huge wail from the back of the room. Kyle. As Ben watched, Kyle's voice ramped up an octave and his wail became a scream that went on and on and on. He was staring at an ant farm. No one was near him. Ben couldn't see any blood or any sign that his son was hurt. Kyle just kept staring at the ant farm, screeching and flapping his arms.

Ben was frozen to the spot, but not Ms. Nicols. She brushed past him, muttering as she went, "Oh no, he's not like these kids. None of them is screaming over an ant farm."

Ben clenched his teeth and strode after the teacher. She had already turned Kyle around so he was no longer facing the ants. She was speaking softly to him but Ben couldn't make out the words. She put her hands on Kyle's shoulders and pushed down. Hard.

"Hey!" Ben protested.

He reached to interfere, but something amazing happened. Kyle stopped. His screeching actually stopped at her touch. After a few more seconds, he sort of melted into his new teacher, allowing her to stroke his hair. He never let Ben touch him like that.

The principal turned to Ben. "You were saying…?"

Ben had not gotten as far as he had in business without holding his ground. Something about this Ms. Nicols got under his skin. "I'd really prefer my son be in another class, a normal one. And one with a different teacher. Aren't kindergarten teachers supposed to warm and nurturing? While I'm sure Ms. Nicols has her good points, warm and fuzzy she isn't."

Ben and the principal both turned to look at the teacher. As she walked toward the carpet area in the corner of the room, two children ran up to her, each hugging her from a side. She wrapped an arm around each child, smiling down at them as they walked.

"Well, she certainly wasn't warm to me," Ben complained.

"Jordan," Ms. Nicols called, "please get Mr. Wickens something to sit on. The Hokki™ behind my desk would work."

A grinning five year old half dragged, half-carried a bright green stool across the room towards Ben. Ben moved to reach for it, but the boy twisted his body between Ben and the stool, saying, "I can do it." Ben let him. The child proudly placed it in front of Ben who stared at it. He was sure it would crumple under his weight, plus there was obviously something wrong with it. Where it should be flat on the ground, it wasn't, well flat on the ground. It listed seriously to one side. Ben tried righting it, but the stool swayed to its other side. The little boy giggled.

Ben asked, "What am I supposed to do with it?"

"You sit on it, silly!" The child thought his question preposterous. "Like this." He swung his hip over the top and tried perching on the too tall stool, without either foot hitting the ground, the hopped off.

Cautiously, Ben lowered his bottom to the chair, keeping most of the weight on his feet. It was uncomfortable and awkward. The other woman in the room, Ben forgot her name, took pity on him and assured him that it would hold his weight. Ben tried. There was no cracking sound of breaking plastic and he was not flat on the floor. So far, so good. He cautiously allowed himself to relax and found that he swayed a bit himself. After the first few minutes, it wasn't so bad. He could actually rock back and forth or side to side.

Ben felt eyes on him. A tiny girl in torn jeans watched him. "Are you afraid when it wobbles?" she asked.

"Ah, well, not really afraid. I wasn't sure it would be strong enough to hold me. It's not so bad, though." Then he noticed what she was sitting on. What in the world?

"I like my chair better than a Hokki™," she informed him.

"What exactly is it you are sitting on?"

The child looked at him like he was daft. "It's called a stool."

It was not like any other stool Ben had ever seen. Sure, it had a round piece of wood to sit on, but the thing had only one leg. He looked closer. The single leg was in the middle, so it was doubtful it had simply lost its other three legs. As he watched, the child wiggled on the stool, humming to herself as she drew with crayons.

"Why does your teacher make you sit on that?" he asked.

"Make?" she looked puzzled. "She doesn't make us sit on anything. We choose which way we want to sit. Molly, my best friend always likes a peanut and Jaden likes the disc."

"Why? Why don't you just sit on regular chairs?"

Another little girl came bouncing by. She made her way across the floor bobbing up and down, sitting on a ball. Actually, a ball with feet and a handle. As she scooted by, she said, "Because it makes my engine run just right."®

Dr. Hitkins came to his rescue. His head was boggling.

"It looks like Kyle is settling in. Do you want to leave him here for the day or would you prefer he start school tomorrow? If you want my opinion, I'd say that we should dive right in and begin today. Otherwise he might get the idea that he comes here just for a half hour or so then goes back home."

Ben cast a guilty look at his son. In the last five minutes, he had not given Kyle a thought. He'd just tried to assimilate what was happening in this strange classroom. "I do need to get to work," he said. "Do you really think Kyle will be all right if I leave him?"

"Spoken like a first time parent. Yes, he'll be fine. We have your contact numbers, so if there is any problem we'll be in touch with you. Where is Kyle's lunch?"

"Lunch?" Cripes. Packing a lunch for his son had not even entered his head.

"Don't worry. We have plenty we can give him today, but you'll need to get him a lunch kit so he can bring his lunch tomorrow."

Ben walked over to Kyle, hesitant to disturb him when he seemed so engrossed in the wooden blocks. He also wasn't sure what to say to him. It's not as if Kyle would miss him when he left; he hardly even knew his father. Ben tried to get Kyle's attention but Kyle did not look up from his blocks. Ben crouched down beside his son and tried to get in his field of vision. He was self-conscious with both Dr. Hitkins and Ms. Nicols watching him, and judging his every move, he felt. So, he spoke to the top of Kyle's head, saying, "Dad's going to work now. You'll be fine here with your teacher and the other kids. I'll come get you after school." No response. With as much of his dignity intact as Ben could muster, he retreated to the door.

When he was almost there, a little voice said, "Bye. See you soon raccoon."

Ben whipped around, but Kyle's head was once again focused on his blocks. But Dr. Hitkins and Ms. Nicols had heard the words and were both smiling at him. Both. This was the first time Ms. Nicols had directed anything but a scowl in his direction. She was actually quite pretty when she smiled.

CHAPTER 3

Having a kid was certainly different. He had heard expecting couples say how having a baby was not going to change their life style. The baby would fit into their lives. Huh. Maybe that was true with babies, but it certainly was not true with five year olds. Or, maybe it was just his five year old, or maybe, it was just him. Once he got the hang of this fatherhood thing, it might be better and he'd have more time.

How did the time get away from him? Usually Ben saw himself as an organized guy, working six, often seven days a week with ten or twelve hour days. He got a lot done. He'd actually liked his life.

As a hand moved a piece, Ben's attention returned to the chess board in front of him. Kyle watched the board intently. Son of a ..... Kyle had just blocked Ben's queen. Bested by a five year old?

"Nice job, little man. But that's it for now. I have to get some work done." Usually Sundays were spent at the office. He motored through paperwork when it was quiet and there were no distractions. This was his first weekend as a father and Ben found that small boys, even ones who didn't talk, took up a lot of time. Exhausting time. Ben had fallen into a doze on the couch when he felt a weight fall into his lap. He woke with a start as the onyx chess men dropped onto his legs. Somehow Kyle had managed to carry the heavy, carved set from its display case across the room to the couch. That set had cost him a fortune. Was he going to have to childproof his home?

"Kyle, no. That's for adults only. You have your own toys; this is daddy's." His words had fallen on deaf ears as Kyle, ignoring him, set the marble board on the coffee table and one by one, fished the fallen pieces off the couch and placed them in their correct places on the board. Ben's irritation turned to wonder as he watched this small boy. How old had he been when he first learned how to play chess? Ten? Twelve? Is this something five year olds did nowadays?

Ben had read how some people with autism had strong visual memories. Maybe that was it and Kyle remembered the positions of the chessmen and was replicating what he'd seen.

Then Kyle turned the board so the white men were by Ben. He folded his hands and waited, staring at the board. Could the kid actually be expecting them to play a game? Ben moved his rook, just to see what would happen. Kyle hesitated only a couple seconds then made his counter move. Correctly. They each took another turn. The kid did seem to know what he was doing. Just to test it out, Ben moved his bishop straight ahead rather than on a diagonal line. Kyle's hands came up. He flapped. "No, no, no!" he said, with his voice rising with each word.

"Sorry. My mistake." Ben took the bishop back and made a different move. Kyle's shoulders relaxed and they carried on. Is this really what five year olds did these days? Shouldn't Deanna have had Kyle out kicking a ball or playing in a sand box rather than teaching him chess?

In his normal, orderly life, Ben was at his desk each morning by eight at the latest. But, he had to take Kyle to school. The earliest he could do this was at 8:30, as he'd been informed by a grouchy Ms. Nicols when he and Kyle showed up in her classroom at eight o'clock one morning. What was the problem? She was obviously there already. Her frosty voice had told him that she was Kyle's teacher, not his babysitter. She was at work early to prepare for the day. What's to prepare, Ben thought. These are just five year olds. They played all day, didn't they? Boy, she certainly was not a morning person, or perhaps just not a Ben kind of person. She had not warmed up to him, and reserved her smiles only for his son.

So, Ben did not arrive at work until nearly nine o'clock these days. Losing an hour or two out of his morning each day was taking a toll. It's a good thing he had no boss to answer to, that was the beauty of owning your own company. The drawback was that he was in charge and the work still needed to get done.

When he had first realized that he would be spending less time at the office now that Kyle was his responsibility, he thought he'd simply carry his work home and do it there. Kyle kept to himself and they'd each do their own thing, right? Little did Ben know. There was always some crisis. A kid needed to eat on time and good food, not just any old thing he could rummage from the fridge. Although Kyle seemed self-sufficient and self-absorbed, he still needed attention and watching. The hours slipped away and little work got done.

Small children slept a lot, didn't they? If Kyle was in bed early, that would leave hours each night for Ben to get caught up. But putting Kyle to bed and getting Kyle to sleep were two different things. Last night's bath was an example.

Personally, Ben preferred showers. They were quick and efficient. He tried the same thing with his son.

The first night he'd carefully set the shower's water temperature, making sure it would not be too hot for a child. Then he'd steered Kyle into the bathroom and told him to get in. Ben then left to get some work done. His concentration was interrupted by a rhythmic bang, bang, bang. He checked the bathroom, only to find Kyle, fully dressed, pulling the sliding shower door back and forth along its runners. Each time he opened it, water spilled out on the floor and on Kyle, who seemed oblivious.

"Kyle, quit it. Can't you see the mess you're making? Look at this floor." Kyle continued opening and closing the door as if Ben wasn't even there.

"Kyle!" Ben's hand stopped the door and pulled it closed. "Look at me. Kyle, get into the shower while I clean up the floor."

Ben reached for towels and bent to mop up the spreading flood. The shower door opened. Ben felt water on his back and turned. "Now what, Kyle?"

Kyle was standing in the tub, fully dressed, and scrunched into a corner, cowering from the water flow. "Oh, for...." Ben began. He shut off the tap and regarded his son, trying to hold in his temper. Then he remembered. He'd read that people with autism tended to take things literally. Ben had told Kyle to get in. Had he told him to take his clothes off first? Doubtful. Ben sighed.

He hauled his son out of the shower but at least Kyle didn't scream at his touch this time. Ben stripped the sodden clothes off his son, no easy task as each garment clung to the little body. Kyle stood still, not helping but not resisting either.

Ben debated skipping the whole business but as he pulled off Kyle's socks, his nose was near Kyle's head. His hair didn't have that clean, little boy smell, but more of a sweaty overtone. He needed a scrubbing. For that matter, so did Ben.

What the hell. He'd kill two birds with one stone. Guys showered beside each other in locker rooms all the time. Ben stripped, then turned on the shower again. He stepped into the water flow then reached for Kyle. As usual, Kyle went stiff, holding his body as far from Ben's as he could. Obviously this child was not exactly warming up to his father yet. He plunked Kyle in front of him, under the full force of the water. Ben felt Kyle take in a big breath. Ben knew this routine - Kyle was preparing to let out one of his horrendous screams. Ben grabbed Kyle under the arms and spun with him, settling him near the back of the tub where Ben's body would shield Kyle from most of the water flow.

Not knowing what else to do, Ben massaged Kyle's shoulders the way he had seen Ms. Nicols do. As Kyle tensed, he remembered how firmly she'd pressed, not the light touch he thought you'd use with a small child. As he pressed harder, he felt Kyle relax. Ben stepped to the side so the edges of warm water flow touched Kyle. Ben relished the quiet, the warm water and steam and a few peaceful moments with this little man. His son.

Then, he remembered his duty as a father. Nice as this moment was, he needed to get his son clean before the hot water ran out. He reached for the shampoo, warmed it in his hands then began massaging Kyle's scalp. He rubbed gently, softly, watching the suds. Out of nowhere, Kyle stiffened then let out this blood-curling scream.

"What, what?" Ben cried. He could not see anything wrong. He turned Kyle to face him and saw the shampoo suds flowing down Kyle's forehead and into his eyes. Kyle's balled fists punched at his eye sockets. Frantic, Ben pulled Kyle's hands from his face and held them. How the hell would he get the shampoo out of the kid's eyes? Didn't he know enough to shut his eyes when his hair was being washed?

Ever tried to pry a child's eyes open? Wet eyelids and cheeks are slippery, no less slippery with a hysterical, soapy child. Ben tugged the squirming ball of boy under his arm, stepped out of the shower and held Kyle's head under the sink's tap. He turned the water on and tried to fit the boy's head under the flow. Not going to work. He sat Kyle on the vanity and reached for a glass. Holding his head over the sink, he carefully poured water across his eyes. Gradually Kyle stopped howling. Ben had no idea if the crying had washed the shampoo from his eyes or drenching them with water had worked. Either way, this crisis seemed over. Ben let the tension in his shoulders relax. As he turned around, his feet squelched in water. Only then did he notice the steady stream of water running from the shower faucet onto the floor. "Son of a ...."

CHAPTER 4

I t all came down to money, didn't it? As an accountant, that belief framed the basis of his work life and his personal life. That was part of the reason he wanted no part of his father's bakery. The thing had been leaking money for years.

Money came easy to Ben. At thirty-three, he worked hard, lived simply and didn't have a lot of needs, with just one real indulgence - the sound system set up in his living room. His business was flourishing. There was no way it shouldn't with the hours Ben put in. Even in tough economic times, accounting firms were still in demand.

Ben's bank account had looked healthy until that call came from Deanna about Kyle. But that certainly changed after he paid Deanna for back child support since Kyle's birth, and put another ten thousand into a registered education plan for Kyle's college. Then, each month he put money into the college fund and two thousand for the ABA treatments. He would have been able to handle that on top of his condo fees and payment, if it wasn't for that damn bakery. It was bleeding him dry. There had to be a doorway out of this.

Even worse, it had to remain a secret. His father, a Polish immigrant and the technical owner of the bakery had no head for books and no idea that what he took in did not cover what needed to go out each month. Some months were better than others, but Ben always had to contribute something, whether for employee salaries or bills left over at the end of the month. If only the old man would listen or admit that he could no longer run the place and let his daughter, Ellie, take over formally. Hell, she had run the place for years with their father there only as a figurehead.

You can only whittle away at your savings so long until the word savings was an oxymoron. Prior to Kyle coming to live with him, it had not been such a worry. When Ben needed to make more money, he just worked more. Simple. Maybe it wasn't much of a life, but it was his life and it had seemed to work for him and those around him.

With Kyle to look after, it was not so easy to put in all those work hours. For one small boy, he certainly took up a lot of time. Since his office was in the same building as his condo, Ben was used to slipping back to the office after supper and at any hour to get more work done. Now, he couldn't leave Kyle alone in the condo to go to the office. He'd tried taking Kyle with him last night, but ended up spending more time looking at Kyle than at his ledgers.

Then he'd tried packing up his files to work on them at home. After all, kids slept a lot, didn't they? Apparently Kyle had not read that book because he sure as heck didn't seem to sleep the way Ben imagined kids were supposed to. But there did come a time each night when Kyle was in bed and asleep. That was when Ben thought he'd get work done. Last night he'd come to with his head on his desk and drool on his papers. Having a kid around was exhausting.

Now, the crunch was on. The bakery's mortgage was due next week. Actually, it's second mortgage. Neither Ben nor his sister knew why their father had re-mortgaged the bakery when surely it had been almost paid off. But, he'd done it and there was no money to make this quarterly payment. Ben to the rescue, he thought, mocking himself. Only this time, there was no money in

Ben's account either. So, he'd need to work like a demon this week to finish these contracts and get the payments in his account so he could get the funds to his sister. That meant long hours, the kind of hours he'd been used to putting in pre-Kyle.

Kyle was at school and Ben was at his desk. He thought about it. Four little words - Kyle was at school. That sounded so simple but hell, it was not. Getting one small boy up, ready and to school took more organizational skills than Ben certainly possessed. He ran a business with ten employees, handled million dollar accounts, but could not manage one small boy.

They'd been late for school today. The frosty Ms. Nicols certainly let him know what she thought of that. At least she had smiled at Kyle and welcomed him even if she did block his father at the door. But, he was safely at school now and Ben could concentrate on his business.

He worked through lunch, focusing and motoring through the files on his desk. He checked the work of his subordinates, lined up meetings with potential new clients and ploughed through the reports. Lucky for Ben, when he was in the zone he could really work. The rest of the world dropped away from him.

His phone rang and he glanced at the caller ID. Beside the ID was a clock. Son of a ..... It was three thirty. School was over at three fifteen and he should have been there to get Kyle. This call was about a merger he was brokering, one that would net him a nice chunk of change.

Ben rubbed his hands over his face. Well, the priority was Kyle. He phoned the school secretary to see if Kyle was all right. Her normally cheery voice was a notch colder than usual. If he'd hang on, she'd find out. Yes, she came back on the phone; Kyle was waiting in his classroom. All the other children had been picked up. There was censure in her voice. Ben apologized and said someone would be right there. He hung up on her voice.

What to do, what to do. Send his secretary after Kyle? Kyle didn't know her and might freak out. Didn't they teach kids about stranger danger or some such thing?

Millie! It came to him. Millie was the perfect answer. Kyle had already met his cleaning lady and today was Millie's day to be at his condo, cooking and cleaning.

Ben called his home. "Millie, I need a big favor. Kyle is still at school and I can't get away to go pick him up. Would you be able to go to the school and get him for me? Then stay with him till I get home around say six thirty?"

There was a pause. What was wrong? Millie was always so accommodating.

"Mr. Wickens, I'm sorry but I don't think that's possible."

"What? Why not? It's just this one time. Kyle's a little boy and he's left at school waiting for someone to get him."

"I understand that and I feel for the tyke but I'm afraid I have other commitments."

"Other commitments? What do you mean?"

"I mean that when I'm finished with your place I have another job. I was just packing up to leave. If I don't go right away, I'll miss the bus and not get this next job done before dark."

"Ah, Millie, look. I'll pay you double if you'll just do this for me today."

Millie sounded miserable, but remained firm in her refusal.

Ben hung up, rubbed his face some more, then picked up his car keys and headed out the door.

How did parents do this day after day? Ben was late again, twenty-five minutes late to be exact. Honestly, today he hadn't forgotten about picking Kyle up from school, not like the other day. And, he would have been on time, too, if he had not picked up the ringing phone just as he was leaving the office. The phone call actually hadn't taken that long, but then traffic had been detoured and it all added up to him being late.

He strode quickly into the office, needing to leave his completed registration form with Marie, the secretary. Marie glanced at him then at his side. Not seeing his son, she asked, "Where's Kyle today?"

"Still in his classroom. I was late getting here."

Marie's welcoming smile faded. "Oh, dear. That's not good. Kids thrive on routine and things like this can really throw them off."

Thanks for that, Ben thought. Then, something about the way Marie was looking at him, something about the way she tilted her head reminded him of something. Or someone. "Have we met before?" he asked her, "I mean before this week."

"No, I don't think so. I might remember you, but I usually don't forget kids once I've met them."

"It's just that you remind me of someone, but I can't think of where we might have met. But, I'd better go collect Kyle now."

At least all was quiet as he approached the kindergarten classroom. There was a murmur of voices. Not wanting to disturb them, Ben poked his head in the doorway. There, nestled on the bean bag chair were Kyle and Ms. Nicols. She was reading him a book and their heads were close together as they studied the pictures. Kyle rested trustingly against her.

Ben felt a jab of resentment. Why was Kyle so relaxed with her when he was so jumpy around him, his father? Why did Kyle snuggle willingly against her, yet tense when Ben came close. He was trying, wasn't he? What did it take to open the door and win this kid over?

As Ben watched, the teacher tussled his son's hair and Kyle leaned into her. Ben's teeth clenched. He wanted that kind of closeness with Kyle but it didn't seem that the kid shared his wishes. Why did Kyle relish this closeness with a virtual stranger when he couldn't stand his own father's touch?

36

Ben spoke more sharply than he intended, his annoyance and hurt clear in his voice. His intrusion into the cozy scene startled Kyle. This earned a glare from Ms. Nicols. Figures. That's all he ever seemed to get from her.

The teacher looked toward Lori, the EA or Educational Associate in the room. Ben had gathered that she had some training in education but not as much as a teacher and definitely not as much as Ms. Nicols. But, the two operated as a seamless team in the room. In fact, if you didn't know for sure who the teacher was and who the assistant, it would be hard to tell. Sometimes Ms. Nicols stood at the front of the room directing the whole group; sometimes Lori took that role while Ms. Nicols worked with an individual or small group.

Now, Lori walked with Kyle toward the cubby where his coat and backpack hung. She talked with him while he put his belongings in his back pack.

Ms. Nicols rounded on Ben. She crooked her finger at him, beckoning him back into the hall and shut the door.

"Do you know what time school is out?"

Ben figured this was a rhetorical question, but she didn't give him time to answer anyway.

"Do you have any idea how it felt to Kyle to watch everyone else's family pick them up? To be the only student left behind?"

Ben had not thought of it that way. He'd assumed that the teacher was mad that she'd had to look after Kyle for a few extra minutes. He couldn't see what the big deal was since she was obviously there anyway. Now, with a few words, she put a different take on his tardiness. She was right.

Maybe his thought process showed on his face because her tirade softened.

"Routine is so important to kids like Kyle. Look. When you have autism, the world can be a scary place. It can seem that things come at you from all sides. You're contending with the sensory issues when every touch, every sound, every light can feel like just too much."

Ben listened intently, his defensive anger fleeing.

"Then, there's the whole language issue. We live in a talkative world. People with autism spectrum disorders have trouble with auditory processing."

Ben's face showed that he had not a clue what she was talking about.

"What I mean is that while the child can physically hear all right, he will have trouble making sense of what he hears. Remember that teacher in the old Charlie Brown movies? The one who went, 'Wa, wa wa wa wa' and we had no idea what was said? That's how it often is for kids with autism. And, for some, they not only have trouble understanding what is said to them, but they also have trouble letting us know their wants and needs."

Some of this made sense to Ben, but it was a lot to take in.

"There's more. Most of us automatically see patterns and connections in the world and our daily lives. Not so with many kids who have autism. They have to be directly taught that there are patterns and consistencies and you can predict what is going to happen. When you can do that, the world is not quite as scary a place."

Ben tried to follow her words.

"In this classroom we work hard to make it a safe place to come to. To do that, we create routines and make it predictable so that the children don't need to feel on edge all the time, wondering what's coming next and what might be expected of them."

That made sense. Ben liked order himself.

"We have a morning routine and an end of the day routine. You, Mr. Wickens, ruined your son's end of the day routine." She glared at him and continued without mercy. "You should have seen his little face when all the kids were picked up but him. He has not been with you long and he needs to feel secure with you, that he has a place with you and can count on you."

She was right. What could he say?

Ben went to the back of the room where the children's belongings were hung. He took Kyle's coat from its hook and approached his son. Kyle stood passively while Ben awkwardly worked his son's arms into the jacket. He then knelt to do up the zipper.

Melanie called out, "Mr. Wickens, would you please come here a minute."

Ben looked up to see her frowning at him. "In a minute," he said. "I just need to do this for Kyle."

"Now, please." Annoyed, Ben looked back at her. While his attention was diverted, Kyle squirmed, letting the coat dangle off the ends of his arms. Ben sighed at the thought of having to do this all over again.

When he reached her desk, Melanie launched into him, keeping her voice low. "What do you think you're doing?" she asked Ben.

"I'm putting my kid's coat on since we're already late, as you kindly informed me."

"Make him do it himself."

"I'm just getting to know my son. I like doing things for him. Look, I missed his earlier years; I have a lot to make up for."

"This isn't about you, Mr. Wickens. It's about Kyle and what's best for him."

"Are you saying I don't have my own kid's best interests at heart? Besides, he can't do it. He hasn't once put on his own coat since he's been with me."

Melanie turned from Ben to look at Kyle, standing beside a grinning Lori. Kyle's jacket was on and zipped. His shoes were on and done up. His back pack was on and he stood waiting by the door with Lori, the EA. Lori, grinning, assured them that Kyle had done it all by himself.

Late yet again.

Ben had learned something. The words, "Hurry up, we're late!" caused a small boy to dig in his heels and not move. At least this small boy. When you looked at the size of him, what made him take so long to get ready in the morning? Since he bathed before bed, he didn't need to shower in the morning. He didn't have to make breakfast; all he had to do was sit down and eat it. He didn't clean up the kitchen afterwards. He didn't even brush his own hair or figure out which clothes to put on. Ben did all that for him and still Kyle dragged his heels and made them late in the mornings. They both left the house angry and disgruntled.

Now, he half walked, half pulled Kyle down the hallway towards his classroom. He could just imagine the look on Ms. Nicols sour face when they entered, late once again. Since the classroom door always seemed to be open, perhaps he could slip Kyle in quietly without her noticing.

Fat chance. Her eagle eyes were everywhere. She was standing right by the door when they approached. Ben tried to push Kyle into the room, hoping to slip out without having to talk with his son's teacher. Kyle entered the threshold then stopped. Ben's gentle push between his shoulder blades made Kyle cry out. His little body tensed and Ben braced himself for a screaming fit.

Kyle's eyes were on his classmates all sitting in a loose circle on the floor around Lori, the education assistant. Ben could not see what the problem was. He knew Kyle had participated in circle time before. Lori held up a book as she read to the kids. Ben could not even see any scary pictures in the book. What was his problem?

But Ms. Nicols was right there. She knelt in front of Kyle, putting her face in his line of vision, blocking out the sight of circle time. She spoke softly and brought her hands up to rest firmly on his shoulders. Ben could see her hands pressing down.

"Kyle, it's all right. This is circle time. What do you do when you come into the class?"

Kyle gave no reaction, but at least he wasn't screaming.

Ms. Nicols reached for a plastic thing on a string around her neck. It was a pouch holding four pictures. The first was a photo of Kyle at the doorway of the classroom. The second picture was of Kyle hanging up his backpack in his cubby. The third was of his son hanging up his coat. The last one was on Kyle sitting at a table. Ms. Nicols held the pictures in front of Kyle's face and prompted, "What is our morning routine?"

It took a few seconds, but Kyle's eyes ceased their frantic perusal of the room and focused on the pictures in front of him. Ben watched some of the tension leave his little body. He pointed to each picture in turn, then walked toward the cubby that had KYLE written above it. He removed his backpack, then his coat, placing them on the hooks. He then went to sit at a table where the name KYLE was taped in big letters. He stared straight ahead.

Ms. Nicols gave a glare Ben's way and as she walked to Kyle said, "Wait right there."

Again, the frostiness was missing from her voice as she knelt by Kyle and showed him another strip of pictures. Craning his neck, Ben could see that that the top picture was of children sitting in a circle on the floor. Kyle stood up and went with Ms. Nicols to the circle. He sat on the edge of the group with almost two feet between him and the nearest child, but at least he was with the rest of the kids and was not screaming or flapping or any of those things that made Ben cringe.

After watching a few minutes to make sure Kyle was all right, Ms. Nicols turned her icy gaze to Ben once more. She marched past him into the hallway, beckoning for Ben to follow her. After checking again to make sure Kyle was all right, Ben complied. He felt like a small boy being sent to the principal's office.

"Just what do you think you're doing to Kyle?" She launched her attack.

How should he respond to that? "I'm bringing him to school," Ben replied as evenly as he could.

"You're late!"

As if he didn't know. "I'm aware of that Ms. Nicols. I can assure you it's not intentional. I'm not used to being late for anything. We start out early, but have you ever tried to get a little boy ready and out the door on time?"

Ms. Nicols' face softened just a tad. "Look. I know you're new to this. Do you want some help?"

Was she offering to come get Kyle up in the mornings? Doubtful. But yeah, he could certainly use any help he could get. Ben nodded for her to continue.

"How do you handle things in the morning? What do you do?"

Ben's defenses came up again but he tried tamping them down for the sake of his son. What they were doing was not working obviously and it made both him and Kyle upset.

Ms. Nicols launched in. "Did you see what happened to Kyle when he came in? He froze at the door. You upset his routine. What was going on in the class was not what he expected to see when he arrived. We can't hold up the program because one child does not arrive on time. We work hard to get our children settled in to a pattern, to make life predictable for them. Predictable means safe in the mind of a child, especially a child who has an autism spectrum disorder."

Ben interrupted, "But I never said he had..."

The teacher cut him off. "If it looks like a duck and quacks like a duck.....Look. The medical reports have arrived. Remember you gave your wife permission to send them to us?"

"I don't have a wife."

"Your ex-wife, then."

"I don't have an ex-wife, either."

That gave Ms. Nicols pause. Then she carried on. "Whatever. The reports clearly state that your son has autism." Another pause. "He is your son, isn't he?"

Ben's teeth clenched. "Yes, he's my son."

"Your son has autism - the big "A". That's neither the end of the world, nor a death sentence. It simply means he has a different take on the world. He will need to learn strategies to help him make his way. Right now we have no idea just how far he will go. But, you can play a big part in helping him."

"How? I'll do anything I can to help Kyle."

Just the opening the teacher wanted. "To start with, get him to school on time." She paused to let that sink it. "It's not just for my convenience. It throws Kyle when he gets here late; you saw that yourself. It takes time to get him settled in. If he just arrived when all the other children do, it will be easier for him."

"I get that," Ben admitted, "but how? I try. We start early but getting him ready and out the door is not easy, short of dragging him."

"How do you get him ready?"

Ben looked at her.

"Tell me what your morning routine looks like."

"Routine? Well, there's not much of a routine. I used to have a routine when I lived alone, but Kyle, well, he's not much of a routine kind of guy."

"That's where you're wrong," Ms. Nicols informed him. Figures, Ben thought. She continued, "Kyle right now may be unable to establish a positive routine on his own, but he'll flourish with routine. You have to create the structure and impose it". She let him ponder that a moment.

Then, she looked up at him. "I bet you talk a lot, don't you?"

Ben stared at her.

"Tell me what you say to Kyle in the morning."

Ben's frustration showed in his words. "I have to tell him over and over to do every little thing. I know he can dress himself, yet he'll have one sock part way on, then spy some toy and start playing. It's the same thing with breakfast. It should take him five minutes to down a bowl of cereal but it can take forty-five minutes. I feel like I have to rag on him all the time to get the simplest thing done." Ben warmed to his subject. "I know it gets on Kyle's nerves and it damn sure gets on mine. It makes him late for school and me late for work. I'm already at my desk an hour later than I used to. I tell him and tell him and tell him but he doesn't listen."

Ms. Nicols nodded. "Look. I'll try to explain. People with autism spectrum disorders, and yes, including Kyle, take in information that they see much better than things that they hear. He's a visual learner, rather than an auditory learner." She waited to see if Ben was following her. He was watching her, but hard to tell how much was sinking in.

She tried again. "Did you see what I did when Kyle came in? Did I talk to him or at him? How many words did I use?"

She carried on before Ben could think of an answer.

"I could tell that he was feeling overwhelmed and close to a melt-down So, I didn't talk or give all those verbal explanations I could have. Instead, I showed him. Remember that he learns more easily visually? I showed him pictures of what he needed to do. Did you see how he reacted?"

"Yeah. He followed along and did what he was supposed to. But, he's a little kid and you're his teacher. At his age, teachers are gods and he'll do what you say."

"The key is, I didn't say anything. If I had talked at him, the likelihood of him melting down would have been high. You could see that he was on the verge, couldn't you?"

"Oh, only too well do I know the signs and what happens."

"It's nice that you think I have some marvelous bag of tricks being a teacher, but no, Kyle did not follow the routine because I'm his teacher. He followed because he could understand what was expected of him because I showed him the visuals. This is not the first time he's seen those particular pictures. Look around - they are all over the room."

Ben looked and she was right. He'd not paid attention before, but yes, similar pictures were all over.

"Our classroom runs on routines. These routines are taught using pictures. If you tried this at home, it would make your mornings run more smoothly."

Ben looked skeptical.

"Do you want a hand with this? Are you willing to try?"

Ben's back was up again. What did she think he was?

"Despite what you think of me, if it'll help my son, I'm game."

A smile crept out. That was the first time she'd actually smiled at Ben. He stared at her and caught a glimpse of why the kids gravitated to this woman.

"I have to get back to my class, but here's some paper. Make a list of the things you want Kyle to do in the morning. Leave it on my desk and I'll try to have some visuals ready for you when you pick him up this afternoon. And remember, when you use them, if you use them, stop nagging. Show him, don't tell him." She turned her back on him and the kids made room for her in their circle.

She really did rub him the wrong way, Ben thought. It was a while since he'd met a woman who had such a lousy opinion of him, without even knowing him. He looked around for someplace to sit. The only options close to her desk seemed to be a gigantic beach ball or another of those Hokki™ stools he'd tried that first day. If he'd worried about that holding his weight, the ball looked even more precarious. He'd be damned if he'd fall on his butt in front of her. He gingerly lowered himself to the Hokki™ and wiggled to get comfortable. He looked up and caught Ms. Nicols watching and suppressing a smile. Lori, the EA did not even attempt to hide her grin. Ben sighed and got on with his assigned homework.

"How'd it go this morning?" A less antagonistic Ms. Nicols approached Ben when he came to pick up Kyle after school several days later. They had made it on time this morning and Kyle had easily slipped in with the other kids, without freezing at the door.

"Not perfect, but better, certainly better. Thanks. Your cards helped."

Ben had remembered her admonishment that the cards were not miraculous and Kyle would not automatically know what they meant. Ben would first have to teach him. Ben had wanted to tell Ms. Nicols that she was his teacher, that Ben did not have time to teach. But since she'd gone to all this work for him, he should keep his mouth shut and just give it a try. It couldn't be worse, could it?

And, it actually had helped. Surprise, surprise. After supper Ben had taken out the cards. Ms. Nicols had given him a length of cardboard. Running the length of the page was a strip of Velcro. On the back of the card was an envelope and in the envelope were cards, each with matching Velcro hooks. After sorting through them, Ben had shown each to Kyle. He started with the pictures of socks, underwear, pants and shirt, explaining to Kyle that this was how he was to get dressed. Keeping in mind that Ms. Nicols had said not to overwhelm Kyle with a list that was too big, he started first with the things Kyle would need to do to get dressed.

Overseeing the process, Ben had removed each picture as Kyle completed that job and placed it in the envelope. When he was dressed and Ben told him, "All done," Kyle had actually replied. It was not loud, but Ben was sure he heard Kyle say, "Good job."

Encouraged, they had moved on to the bathroom. There Ben placed on the card the pictures of a toilet, hands washed, a face being washed, and teeth brushed. Again, it worked, with only a minimum of coaching from Ben. He saw Kyle looking over at the cards to see what came next. And, the last picture Kyle removed himself and placed it in the envelope.

Then, on to the kitchen and breakfast. Again, it worked but not quite as slickly. There were distractions and Kyle would rather play with his cereal than eat it. Still, they did not end up mad at each other as they had the other mornings. Instead of ragging on Kyle to get moving, Ben just tapped the appropriate card to draw his son back to the task at hand. It worked! There was actually something to this shut-up-and-show business.

But, Ben needed to learn more. He had not quite gotten the order correct. Tomorrow, he would not have Kyle get dressed and washed before he ate. By the time most of the cereal was inside Kyle, a fair bit was on his outside as well. His face needed washing again and he needed a change of shirt. Kyle protested. Ben could see his point. According to the visual schedule, he had already done those things and put their pictures away in the envelope. Kyle might be learning, but Ben obviously needed to learn more as well.

Ben watched as the kids formed a line and one by one trailed past their teacher. Ms. Nicols addressed each child as they went out the door. "High five or hand shake or a hug?" she asked each. This intrigued Ben.

"Why do you ask them that?"

"I want to make a connection with them as they leave for the day. You may have noticed that some kids are naturally more physically affectionate than others. Some want a hug. Others don't like that kind of contact and may not even want to touch hands. But shaking hands and some degree of physical contact is part of our culture, so we teach them to do one of these at the end of each day. Some stick with one choice; others vary it day to day."

"I notice that you hug like you mean it."

"Are you suggesting that I'm not gentle?" Ms. Nicols grinned at him, knowing she was putting him on the spot.

The smiling Ms. Nicols was a far cry from the stern, condemning Ms. Nicols Ben had met only a week or so ago. He squirmed a bit. "Well, these are just small children and you do seem to squeeze them rather tightly."

"There's a reason for that. Have you noticed how we touch your son?" Ben nodded and she continued. "Many kids with autism spectrum disorders have sensory sensitivities. To them, running hand gently down their arm may feel to them what fingernails on a chalkboard may to you. But if your touch is firmer, it can have a calming effect. Haven't you experienced that with Kyle?"

"Yeah, I have. The first night he was with me, when I touched him I did it with kid gloves. He pulled away and that could be just enough to start up his screeching." Ben grimaced at the memory. He'd been convinced his kid hated him and could not stand his touch. "But if I put my hand firmly on his shoulder to guide him somewhere, he allows it."

From the look Ms. Nicols gave him, he expected to be patted on the head or given a gold star. But he did feel proud of himself. Maybe he could get the hang of this parenting this after all. And, he had been wrong about Ms. Nicols. Her students liked her, his son liked her and he was starting to himself.

Ben made it on time to pick up Kyle. Well, almost. It truly was hard to get out of the office at precisely the right time each day. He should never have answered that last phone call.

As he approached the kindergarten room, he heard screams. He stopped. Kyle! Those were Kyle's cries. What was that woman doing to him? Had Ben's first impression been right and she should not be allowed near his son?

Rushing into the room, he spied his son on the floor. Kyle was tossing his head back and forth, kicking his heels and screaming. Ms. Nicols stood beside him placidly as if nothing was wrong. Lori was also nearby, but tidying a book rack rather than attending to his son. Three other kids were putting on their coats and one mother waited nearby.

"What the hell's going on here?" Ben yelled. "What's wrong with my son?"

"Nothing, Mr. Wickens. And, please keep your voice down," said Ms. Nicols.

"Why aren't you helping him? What's wrong with Kyle?"

"He's mad."

"Mad? At what? Did someone hurt him?"

"He wants Jordan's Dora book," the teacher explained.

"Then give it to him," Ben said. What was wrong with these women?

"Excuse me? Give it to him? It doesn't belong to him."

"So?" Ben said. "I'll buy the kid another one. Or two if he wants. Just give that one to Kyle."

Ms. Nicols turned on him. "This isn't about buying anyone anything. Money can't fix everything. This is about Kyle throwing a tantrum to get what he wants."

"If you just give it to him, he'll stop this god awful screaming," said Ben.

"It's not his book. He didn't ask to borrow it; he didn't want to share. He snatched it out of Jordan's hands. We don't tolerate that behavior in this class."

Kyle had quieted for a minute, listening to the exchange between his father and his teacher. On hearing Ms. Nicols' last words, he squirmed sideways and tried to kick her.

"Kyle!" Ben was horrified. He started to apologize to the teacher but she held up her hand to stop him. They watched as Kyle leapt to his feet, ran to the front of the room and attempted to tear the papers from the wall. Lori, the EA was there and effectively blocked him before he did too much damage. He raised his foot to kick her. She said his name firmly and crouched down in front of him, placing her hands on his shoulders. Looking him in the eye, she pressed firmly. It took a few seconds, but before their eyes, they could see the tension drain out of his little body.

"Now, shall we clean up these papers?" Lori asked him.

Kyle bent and picked up the scraps he'd torn and carried them to the waste basket.

Ben was drained. Kyle seemed to be recovering faster than he was. Ben turned to Ms. Nicols. "What just went on here? Why weren't you helping him? I've seen you do things for other kids when they were upset?"

"What you just witnessed was a tantrum. Kyle was mad because he didn't get his way. Remember how he reacted the first time he saw the ant farm at the back of the room that first day?"

Ben nodded.

"Well," she continued, "that wasn't a tantrum. Your son was genuinely upset then. That was what we call a meltdown. He was feeling overwhelmed for whatever reason. We used some sensory techniques and they helped him to calm down. That's quite different from what just happened here.

Ms. Nicols continued her explanation. "If you or I or anyone had given in to his tantrum and given him what he wanted just because he raised a fuss, then we would have taught him that tantrums are a good way to control others. Pitch a fit and people will give in. Is that the way you want your son to think?"

"I get it," said Ben. "It's just hard to see him like that. And, he almost kicked you. God, I'm sorry."

She put a hand on his arm and actually smiled. "I'm fine and it's fine. He's just a little boy and he's still learning how to navigate his world. He's already doing better and will continue to do so."

CHAPTER 5

The next day he was late. Again. Only this time he made it on time for school both morning and after school. He, who always considered himself Mr. Punctual and hated lateness in others, was actually late for an important meeting with a new client. A woman Ben had been training, a new hire, was giving her first pitch to a potential client. The firm needed this client, Ben's wallet needed this client and Bonita needed the confidence boost she'd get when her first pitch produced results.

He should not have taken any time to chat with Ms. Nicols when he picked up Kyle, but the time had just flown. Funny how that could happen with that woman, as annoying as she could be. Now, he was once again in the position of hurrying Kyle along, this child who did not like to be pushed. Ever.

It had briefly crossed Ben's mind to get Kyle settled in the apartment with his toys, and then run the three floors downstairs to his office for the presentation. But that thought was fleeting. He could not leave a small boy alone, even if he was in the same building.

"Come on, Kyle. We're late!" Ben regretted the words even as he said them. When had the words "hurry" or "late" even made Kyle move faster? In fact, they seemed to put him firmly into balking mode. Yep, it was happening again. Kyle's feet stuck to the floor. Ben took his arm to move him along faster. Kyle's "No, no, no..." voice started to rise. All right. Deep breath. Try this again.

"Kyle, we're going to daddy's office. There'll be a meeting around a big table. Some important people will be there. See? We've brought your toys. I'll make you a spot in the corner and you can play while the grownups talk. All right? Daddy needs you to be real quiet while we meet."

Kyle neither looked at him nor gave any response. Ben could only hope he'd gotten through.

When they reached his board room, the others were all present. Bonita looked nervous but relieved to see him. Ben entered, holding Kyle's arm, but felt resistance. Kyle was frozen at the doorway. His gaze took in all the strange faces then the floor to ceiling windows overlooking the cityscape outside. Ben felt Kyle tense. When Ben tugged on his arm, Kyle leaned backwards and his mouth opened. No, no not now, not in front of all these people. Please don't pitch a fit.

Ben's anger rose. All he needed the kid to do was to sit quietly and play with his toys for half an hour. Was that expecting too much? He'd just turned his own life upside down to accommodate his son; couldn't the kid do at least a little bit for him?

Ben squatted down to put his face near his son's. Maybe he could reason with him. Too bad he didn't have some visuals in his back pocket this time, but he hadn't thought of it.

Then he looked, really looked at Kyle. This was not a child being stubborn and uncooperative. This was a child who was terrified. His little body was rigid and with such a look of fear on his face. Ben's heart broke. What a bastard he was to be thinking awful things about his son, when the child was clearly scared to death of something.

But what? Yeah, there were strangers here but Kyle had never shown such fear of people before. What was he staring at? Ben followed Kyle's line of sight to the windows. What was there? The glass was clear; there were no birds or planes going by. What was the matter with the kid?

All eyes were on them. If Ben couldn't control his own son, what would the new client think of him? How could he trust Ben with his business if Ben obviously couldn't manage one little boy? His eyes returned to Kyle and all thoughts of business fled his mind. His son was scared, just plain afraid.

Without thinking about those around them, he gathered Kyle close and squeezed tight. He hid Kyle's face against his shirt to blot out whatever it was that frightened him. He rocked him back and forth, brushing firmly up and down his back the way he'd seen Ms. Nicols do with upset students. Gradually Kyle's steel rod of a spine started to relax. His little body shuddered as he surrendered his weight to Ben's arms. Despite the situation and all the eyes on them, Ben felt a thrill. *My son trusts me. I was able to calm him down. Maybe the kid likes me, even a little.*

Someone above him cleared a throat. Ben raised his head to meet Bonita's gaze. She was nervous about interrupting him but probably anxious to get her meeting underway.

"I'll just get Kyle settled. You go ahead and start and I'll be right in."

Ben lifted Kyle into his arms and turned back into the hallway. What to do, what to do?

"Are you feeling better now, buddy? What was it that bothered you?" There was no response. This was worse than charades because then at least your partner tried to give you some clues to work with.

Maybe if Kyle just sat on Ben's lap, they could get through this. Ben started through the door with Kyle in his arms. He made it only a couple steps when Kyle raised his head, saw the windows and let out a god awful shriek. Bonita, who had just started her power point presentation dropped the remote with a clatter to the table. That sound though, was hardly heard over the cries coming from Kyle. He began writhing in Ben's arms making it difficult to hold onto him. God, Ben thought, if I drop him, he'll really have something to howl about. How could one forty pound child be so difficult to hold?

Ben sat down across from the windows and placed Kyle on his lap facing him. He wrapped Kyle's legs around his waist and again tucked his son's face into his shirt. He held on tight to the little boy. The shrieks started to subside once again, and then became whimpers.

Ben raised his head to find all eyes on them. What to say, how to explain? Damned if he should have to apologize about his son. This was his company and everyone in the room was either his employee or a potential client. If they didn't like his son, they could leave. He and Kyle weren't going anywhere.

Some of the eyes looked at him with sympathy. Some showed censure. They probably looked down at him for not being able to control his kid. Or for raising a spoiled brat. But not all the eyes had that look.

Mr. and Mrs. Bower, the new or hopefully new clients didn't look at him that way. Mr. Bower spoke up.

"Is he afraid of heights? I hate these picture windows in sky scrapers myself. I never look out of them."

Was that it? Was Kyle afraid of heights?

Mrs. Bower was the next to speak. "Our grandson has autism. He hates shiny surfaces and anything that reflects the light. I wonder if that's what bothered your little boy."

Ben looked at her. These two strangers, these people who had no blood connection to Kyle and had never met him before, in five minutes had come up with two possible explanations for Kyle's behavior. Ben had been clueless as to what the problem might be.

He looked gratefully at the Bowers. "I'm sorry about the ruckus. I have no idea what set him off, but he was really upset." He thought a second. "You know about autism?"

"Oh, yes. We've learned a lot since our grandson was diagnosed - had to learn. There's a little boy down the street who has autism as well. More than one in every hundred children in our country has autism now."

"Actually, it's now one in eighty-eight," Mr. Bower corrected.

Ben looked at them. He had not known that. One in a hundred? One in eighty-eight?

Bonita looked at him pleadingly. Ben nodded at her to continue. As she talked, Ben again felt Kyle's little body gradually relax. Ben let the tension drain out of his own body. Maybe they'd get through this yet.

Ben whispered to Kyle, "All right now, bud? Do you want to get down and play?" If he set Kyle on the floor by his chair, the center support of the table would block his view of the window. It should be safe.

Ben set Kyle down and opened the backpack of toys. Kyle brought out his little cars and lined them up. There seemed to be some exact order to this that only Kyle knew. But at least it was a quiet activity.

He was concentrating on Bonita's presentation, so the sounds didn't register at first. They were coming from near his feet. It was Kyle. He was singing:

"Do-do-do-do-do-Dora!

Well, even if it was nonsense he was singing, at least it was quiet and he wasn't screaming.

Kyle continued, getting a little louder all the time.

"Do-do-do-do-do-d Dora!

Do-do-do-do-do-Dora!" Ben tried shushing him. "Sh! Kyle! Quietly, please."

"Dora dora dora the explorer!

Boots that super cool exploradora!"

"Kyle, hush. Keep it down," Ben said, his own voice rising

"Need your help!

Grab your backpacks!

Let's go!

Jump in!

Vámanos! "

Ben's patience was slipping away. "Kyle, stop that right now."

Kyle's voice rose above Ben's, singing, "You can lead the way!" Ben, his face red, apologized to the group, saying he had to take his son out of there. He grabbed Kyle in one arm, the backpack in the other and took long strides to get out of the conference room. Kyle had started his song over again,

"Do-do-do-do-do-Dora!"

But the last "Dora" changed to a shriek as Kyle stiffened in his arms. His arms flailed and Ben had trouble not dropping the squealing, squirming little boy. What now? He turned with Kyle in his arms to survey the spot where they'd been moments before. He's left two of the cars. Ben clenched his teeth together to keep all the bad words in his head. They should not be uttered in a business meeting or in front of a small boy, no matter how trying he was.

Ben stooped with Kyle in his arms swinging Kyle's hands so they could pick up the delinquent cars. Kyle grabbed them and held them to his collar bones. The two of them left the room hurrying toward the elevators and the safety and privacy of their home.

It was not good to resent your kid. Kyle was just being a child, a child with autism and getting by the best he could. Kyle did not intend to ruin Ben's business meeting. It was Ben's fault for subjecting his son to such a situation.

But how did people do it? How did they hold down a job and care for a child? There had to be a better way.

When Ben and Kyle unlocked the door of their condo, tantalizing aromas came from the kitchen. Kyle made a beeline for that room. Ben followed. There they found Millie, his housekeeper. Millie came twice a week to tidy up his place, clean and to cook meals. She was a wonderful cook. She made up two or three meals, kept one warming in the oven and froze the others with instructions on how to heat them up. Weekends he was on his own, but Ben appreciated this amount of help, especially now that he had Kyle to think about.

"You sit yourself right down here, little man. I just baked some chocolate chip cookies for you." Kyle plunked himself down in anticipation. Ben did the same. He may not be that little, but he certainly craved Millie's cooking.

Once Kyle finished and went off to watch another Dora the Explorer™ video, Ben planned what he'd say to Millie.

"Thanks for the cookies and the meals. They're great and Kyle loves them." There. How was that for easing in? Millie regarded him steadily, guessing that more was coming.

Ben rubbed his hands over his face. "Millie, I'm in a bind. I'm not doing well at all and I need to do better for Kyle's sake. Today after I picked him up from school I had to take him back to the office with me for a meeting. It did not go well. I should have known that you can't expect a little boy to sit and play quietly through a dry business meeting. I had to leave early and have one of my assistants carry on without me." He paused with a sigh. Bonita had done just fine and pulled off the deal, no thanks to him.

"This is Year End for some of our biggest clients. In the accounting world, that's a big deal. I can pass some things off to my associates, but other things I just can't. Tomorrow I have to be at a meeting from one to five. I can't get out of it and I can't subject Kyle to that. Or them to him, if it went anything like it did this afternoon. "

He looked at Millie. "I'm asking if you would consider coming in tomorrow afternoon to stay with Kyle." Before she could say whatever she was going to say, he rushed on. "I know, I know. This is not in the realm of the housekeeper duties that you do so well. But you're also good with Kyle. Hell, you're a lot better with him than I am. It would just be until five o'clock.

There's still plenty of daylight left then." He remembered that she didn't like being out after dark.

He could see that she was struggling with this. She was truly a nice lady and seemed to care for Kyle.

"What would it take? I'll pay double your regular rate. Or if you'd rather come Saturday and not one of your usual days next week."

Still Millie hesitated. She hated to admit that the extra money really appealed. But there was that long bus ride home and she did so hate to walk that last little bit in the dark.

"Please Millie. I really need your help."

"Are you sure I'd be free to leave by five o'clock?"

"I promise."

That would leave her about an hour and a half of daylight to get home. Plenty of time. "All right," she said.

"Oh," the relief on Ben's face was palpable. "Thank you. And Kyle thanks you. It means a lot to us that you'd do this."

Later that night when Deanna called to see how Kyle was doing, Ben was honestly able to tell her that things were working out all right. Kyle had little interest in talking to his mother on the phone and set the receiver down to return to his video. Ben started to apologize to Deanna but she said she understood. After they hung up, Ben thought that the one thing he didn't understand was how someone could live with Kyle for five years, turn him over to a virtual stranger, then only call once to check on her son's well-being.

One thing Ben had going for him was his ability to focus. That skill had helped to build his business into the enterprise it was today. Today, he fully gave his attention to the client in front of him and to his assistants at his side. So far the afternoon had been productive as they weeded through the troubles the client put before them. The client stretched and said he needed to take a break.

"How long have we been going at it anyway," he asked Ben.

Ben was wading through a file so one of the others called out the time. Almost half past six. It took a few minutes for that to register, to break through Ben's focus on the task at hand. "What did you say?"

"Six-thirty."

Ben leapt up from his chair. "Six-thirty! My babysitter was only free until five. I completely forgot the time." He threw files into his briefcase. "Bonita, would you mind shutting down for me? I have to go get Kyle."

He left without waiting for a response. He didn't wait for the elevator, but flew up the three flights of stairs to his condo, thankful that at least he lived in the same building. Breathlessly he raced into the kitchen, his tie hanging over his shoulder and his jacket on only one arm.

"Millie, Millie, I'm sorry. I completely forgot the time. I'm sorry. This will never happen again."

Kyle and Millie sat watching a video of Dora the Explorer. She had a crossword puzzle by her side. Millie accepted his apology but she was not happy about it. Ben cursed himself. How could he have done something like this to such a nice woman? And, he'd promised her she could leave by five. Thank god she had stayed with Kyle.

Millie was putting her coat on, a worried look on her face.

"Hold on a minute," Ben told her. "Kyle and I will walk you to your car. It's dark out now."

"I'm quite aware that it's dark out and I don't have a car."

"Then how did you get here?"

"On the bus," she replied.

"Is your car in the garage?"

"I don't have a car."

"Then how do you get here each time? A taxi?"

"Mr. Wickens, do you think I could afford a taxi every time I want to go out? I doubt that. The bus is fine but I do always try to be home before dark." She started out the door.

"Hold on, Millie. Wait a sec. We'll drive you home, but you have to wait until I get Kyle's coat."

"That's not necessary. I'll be fine."

"No. It's my fault you're so late. I apologize, but we will take you home. I don't want you out at some bus stop alone this time of night. Come on bud; let's go give Millie a ride."

With Kyle strapped into his booster seat in the back, they drove through the darkness. The drive took half an hour; how long must it take on the bus? Just how long must this woman take getting to and from her jobs?

"Where are the other places you work? Near my building?"

"One is not too far away, but the other is on the other side of town. That one I still do, but the Gibsons moved away last week. I'm now down to just two contracts - yours and that other one."

"Is that good or bad?"

"Well, it gives me a bit more free time this week but I'll need to find another contract pretty quickly."

They drove in silence as Ben thought.

He needed some more information. "Is the reason you wouldn't stay with Kyle after school because you'd have to take the bus home in the dark?"

"Yes. I don't mind the bus in the daylight, but I don't fancy it after dark. The bus doesn't go far enough and I have to walk the last five blocks."

Ben considered this some more. "What if I asked you to pick Kyle up from school each day and stay with him until half past six, then we drove you home?"

It was Millie's turn to think. "Well, I wouldn't mind on the days I'm working for you, but I need to find work for the other three days. I wouldn't be able to get my cleaning finished on the other side of the city and be at Kyle's school in time to get him."

"Millie, do you really like those cleaning jobs?"

"What do you mean? It's a living and I'm good at it."

"I'm not denying you're good at it. I know only too well how good you are. Look. What do you think about working for me - just me? What if you were at my place Monday to Friday, full-time? Or just afternoons if that's what you want? I'd take you home every night so you wouldn't have to worry about the bus in the dark."

Millie did not know what to say. Some of the clients she'd cleaned for had been slobs. Some were not as nice as Ben and going between houses was tiring. It would be nice to have just one place to think about, one system to remember... one little boy to mother.

She looked at Ben.

Ben thought she needed more convincing. "Look. I'll be out of your way during the day. I get Kyle ready and to school in the mornings. You could come in whenever you wanted as long as you picked Kyle up from school, fed him and stayed with him until I got home. If you were still willing to do the cooking and cleaning you do, or any part of it, I'd be grateful."

She still didn't say anything, but thoughts whirled through her head.

Ben tried again. "I have no idea what the going rate is for child care like this. Name your pay. You're probably more up on these things than I. I need someone and it's you we want. Kyle likes you and trusts you. He doesn't feel that way about many people. Hell, you're better with him than I am, but I'm getting better..."

"Yes." Millie interrupted him.

"What?" Ben said. He didn't think he'd heard it correctly. "Did you say yes?"

"Yes." Millie smiled at him. "I'll take the job."

"Hey, did you hear that bud? Millie's going to be with us." He smiled at her. "Thank you. When can you start?"

"I'll need to give two weeks' notice to the Shermans, but I only go there once a week. So for the next two Wednesdays I can't be at your place or get Kyle, but other than that I can start Monday."

Ben followed Millie's directions the rest of the way, feeling that knot in his stomach release now that he knew he had someone trustworthy to help with Kyle. He started paying more attention to the quiet neighborhood he was driving through. This was a place where families lived. There were shrubs and hedges and bikes on the lawn, hockey nets in the driveways and a lived-in feel to the area.

Two more turns took them to Millie's street and her house. Ben pulled into the double driveway and just looked at her home. It was huge, a beautiful old Victoria with wrap-around porches stretching as far as he could see to the side. "Wow," he said, "what a house!"

Millie got defensive. "I know it needs work. Bill and I bought it so many years ago. We'd hoped to fill it with children but that just never happened. We loved the place anyway."

Ben continued staring and now he picked out more details. One of the steps leading to the front door was missing. The porch roof sagged under the upstairs bay window. The roof shingles he could see from the glow of the streetlight seemed to be more curled than straight as their edges pointed skyward.

Millie watched him take that in. "I know. It needs work. It was easier when Bill was alive; he took care of those sorts of things. He was handy and did them himself. Now everything costs so much."

Ben agreed with her that repairs were costly. He had first-hand knowledge of that with his parents' bakery. "How many bedrooms does this place have?"

"Five, plus an extra one that we turned into a study."

Ben got out and unbuckled Kyle's booster seat. "Come on, bud. We're going to see Millie to the door and make sure she gets in all right." To Millie, he asked, "Don't you leave a light on when you're gone?"

She raised one eyebrow at him. "I thought I'd be home before dark today," she reminded him.

Ben ducked his head in apology. "Yeah, it was my fault. Again, I'm sorry." Then he grinned at her. "But maybe it all worked out since you'll come work for me now." He grabbed Kyle's hand. "Let's go, quick, before Millie changes her mind."

Millie laughed as she said, "Good night Mr. Wickens. See you Kyle."

"Good night and the name's Ben. Right?"

CHAPTER 6

This week had been better than the last. Yesterday when he picked Kyle up from school, Ben had complained to Mel and Lori that it was so hard to get Kyle to let him in. His efforts to bond with his son were showing few results. He wanted even some small sign that the door was cracking open just a bit and he was making progress.

Discouraged, he called to Kyle that it was time to go. Without making eye contact, Kyle walked to the door then stood with his hand out, waiting for his dad to take it. Lori grinned and imitated the sound of a door creaking open.

The wet spot on his chest woke Ben. What the hell? The weight against his left side and under his arm registered. Kyle. He's fallen asleep on him and the wet was Kyle's drool. Funny, but that should have been a turn off. Instead, it seemed part of being a dad. A dad. Who would have thought?

He'd never understood his married friends who went all ga ga when they had children. Sure, you might expect their wives to do so, but these guys, these rugby players? They changed when they had kids. Now Ben had entered that world that had seemed so far out there before. And you know, it wasn't half bad. He could get used to this warm, heavy weight at his side. Maybe the door to the mystery that was Kyle was cracking open bit by bit.

Wait! What was he doing? This was Kyle's second nap within a few hours. Ben remembered what it was like to try to get Kyle to bed when the kid wasn't sleepy. Ben had been exhausted those first few days with Kyle and had needed to hit the bed, whether Kyle wanted to or not.

"Wakey, wakey." No response. "Come on, Kyle, time to wake up. Let's go, let's go to the, to the...." What was he going to do with this kid? But they had to do something and preferably something that would wear him out. In a good way, of course. What did kids do? Ah, they played in the park.

"Up. Now, let's go. We're heading to the park to play."

"Play?" a groggy voice asked.

"Let's wash your face, take a..., well, use the bathroom and get on our way." He led Kyle down the hall.

What was it like out? That was the trouble with a condo. With air conditioning and heating and windows with a fifth floor view, he had little idea of what it was really like outside. When he was a boy, they'd just look outside or open a door or run into the backyard to see. What kind of a life was this for a little kid in a condo?

While Kyle was in the bathroom, Ben checked the weather on the internet. Cool enough for jackets.

"Kyle, go grab your jacket." No response. "Kyle. Your coat." No response. Ben sighed and went to find him.

Kyle was in the den, kneeling in front of the couch looking at a Dora the Explorer book. A nice quiet activity, but that's not what Ben was after right now. "Let's go. Grab your coat." Kyle ignored him. Ben's temper, never too far under wraps, rose. "Kyle!" he said sharply. "Now!" Still no response. Ben strode the few feet and took Kyle's arm. The child started and looked at Ben. Ben's annoyance deflated. Kyle acted like he had not heard him, had been engrossed in his book. Who could get mad at a kid who liked books? Maybe he'd inherited Ben's ability to totally focus on what he was doing. It had worked all right for Ben.

But now, he wanted his kid doing things like running around in the fresh air, playing with other children, kicking through piles of leaves. They needed to get moving to hit the warmest part of this fall day.

Just as he opened his mouth to tell him once again to get his coat on, Ben remembered Ms. Nicols admonishment - show, don't tell. Ok. He had a picture of a coat some place. Ben got his own coat then showed Kyle the picture. Kyle looked from Ben's jacket to the picture and went to the low hook that Ben had installed in the hallway. He struggled into the jacket, doing up the snaps on his own with painstaking concentration. There. They were finally ready.

On the way out the door, Ben reached for his ball cap. The sun looked bright. Kyle stood there watching, and then as Ben went to shut the door, he moved with a wail. What, what now? Ben hadn't touched him. What was the kid's problem? Back in the condo, Kyle raced from room to room, frantic. Ben trailed after him telling him to come. Again, Kyle ignored him. Like what else was new? The den was a mess. Kyle's suitcase contents were strewn all over the floor. Finally Kyle, raking through the piles grabbed something and stood. On his head he placed a miniature ball cap then strode to the door. I'll be damned, Ben thought, following his son into the hallway.

The park was a pleasant five block stroll. Actually, it took much longer to get there than usual as Ben matched his steps to his son's much shorter stride. He was tempted to swing Kyle to his shoulders or give him a piggyback ride, but that hadn't worked so well the last time he tried it.

Once at the park, the noises of the city faded away. It was like a world apart, this oasis of grass and shrubs and trees. Along the west side was a playground with a few older kids. Kyle glanced at them but seemed to have little interest in them or their games. Ben took a seat on a bench. "Go on. Go on Kyle and play," he urged. Kyle stood beside Ben and didn't seem to know what to do with himself.

Maybe he's shy and doesn't want to go by himself. Ben took his hand and walked towards the other kids. When he stopped, Kyle stopped without seeming to notice the older kids playing on the slide. The swings were empty so Ben led him that way. he lifted Kyle onto a swing, admonished him to hold tight and walked behind to give him a push. Kyle stiffened and Ben recognized the signs of an impending howl. He quickly retraced his steps until he was facing him again.

"What's the matter buddy? This is fun. You like the swings, all kids like swings. Look, it's like this. I'll push you gently." He remained facing Kyle and, holding the chains, gently rocked the swing. Kyle slowly relaxed his shoulders. As the gentle back and forth movement continued, Kyle closed his eyes and seemed to fully relax. So did Ben. Crisis averted. But what kid didn't love the playground?

Watching him, Ben was afraid that Kyle was going to yet again be lulled into a snooze. He brought him here for exercise and fresh air to tire the kid out, not send him into napville again.

Ben grabbed his hand and set off at a brisk walk, well aware that Kyle had to hustle to keep up. That was the idea. There were few people in the park, only one woman and her dog over yonder. As their feet trod the leave-strewn path, Ben recalled autumn when he was a kid and all the fun they'd had with leaves. He dropped Kyle's hand and quickly used his feet to scoop leaves into a pile. Then he stepped back and ran through the pile, kicking his feet at he went. He remembered from childhood the brittle crunching as the dried leaves cracked beneath his feet, releasing aromas of soil and sun. He rebuilt the pile, then taking Kyle's hand, pulled the child through the pile. Kyle, looking startled, just ran. Then Ben stopped, turned him around and ran him through again. This time Kyle got it. He kicked his feet as he'd seen Ben do.

This time Ben squatted and used his hands to make a pile. Kyle watched for a second, then made his own pile. Ben said, "Ready? One, two, three!" and he jumped in, kicking leaves everywhere. Kyle laughed. He actually laughed! "More," he said.

Ben raised his head in surprise. It was rare to hear Kyle laugh and even rarer for him to speak. Yes!

"Okay, again, bud. First make your pile." Then, "Ready? One, two, three!" With an echoing, "Three!" Kyle mimicked his dad and they both jumped, scattering leaves everywhere.

The next time, after Ben said, "Ready?" Kyle counted with him. The anticipation was almost as much fun as the jumping and the scattering. Ben felt like a kid himself.

He was glad they were in a secluded part of the park and no one was watching. Whoa. There was that lady and her dog again, coming closer. Well, the hell with what she thought. He was having fun with his son. "Ready? One, two, three!"

The next time, Ben thought he'd mix it up a bit. Just before he said three, he reached down and scooped up a handful of leaves. As soon as they jumped into their piles, Ben added to the fray by throwing the leaves over Kyle's head.

There was silence. Oh, shit, Ben thought. Have I ruined it now? So focused was he on his son that Ben had not noticed the woman drawing up to them. She said, "Sit" to her dog, then reached down into Kyle's pile of leaves, grabbed two handfuls and threw them over her own head.

Kyle stared at her as she laughed. Then he lunged for her, wrapping his arms around her legs. It was Ms. Nicols! She gave Kyle a hug while she laughed, then threw more leaves at him. Then she smiled at Ben. A real smile. There was nothing cynical or dismissive about this one. It was the kind of smile she shared with the kids in her room, but somehow different. It warmed Ben and at the same time froze him to the smile. God. She was beautiful. He'd seen her how many times and never noticed before?

"Can I play, too?" she asked.

"By all means," Ben said and stepped back to give her room to make her own pile of leaves. They each yelled their "One, two three" in unison and jumped and threw leaves at each other.

After a few turns, Ben's attention was drawn to the dog. It was huge to his eyes, at least an eighty pound German Shepherd. Ben knew that not all were the family pet type and not all were used to small children. He edged his body between Kyle and the dog, not taking his eyes off the creature. Obviously he was well-trained because he had not moved since receiving that one "Sit" command. But the dog's body was quivering, either with the desire to play or to attack.

Ben couldn't take any chances with his son. "Shouldn't your dog be tied up or something?"

"Why?

"Well, do you think he's safe? Kyle's pretty small and the dog doesn't know us."

"Are you afraid of dogs, Mr. Wickens?"

Ben grimaced. "No, I'm not afraid but I've got a kid to take care of. And the name's Ben."

Ms. Nicols backed down and smiled. Her crusty parts seemed close to the surface or maybe it was just him that brought that out in her.

"Kyle, come with me," she told his son. Ben tensed and moved to interfere." Trust me, Mr. Wickens. I know what I'm doing."

She led the child by the hand to the great dog whose head was level with Kyle's. His son didn't show the same trepidation Ben felt. Ben stayed at Kyle's side, ready to defend his boy if need be.

"Kyle, this is Max. Max, this is Kyle. Shake hands with Kyle." Max lifted a paw and held it there as Kyle didn't move. He didn't look afraid, more as if he didn't know what to do. Ms. Nicols grasped her dog's paw, shook it twice then let go. "Now you're turn, Kyle. Max, shake a paw"

The dog again held up his paw and this time Kyle grabbed it with his free hand. He shook it up and down forcefully and Ben prepared to lunge, but the only sign that this wasn't according to the script was that the dog wiggled slightly backward. His grin didn't leave his face.

Ms. Nicols continued. "Now hold out the back of your hand so Max can sniff it." Kyle obeyed. After a few sniffs,, the dog licked Kyle's hand and Kyle jerked back then giggled. He slowly offered his hand once again and again, got his hand washed.

Without taking his eyes off the dog's massive head, Kyle groped for Ben's hand. When he found it, he thrust his dad's hand towards the dog's mouth. Ben's hand got a thorough washing as well. Between giggles, Kyle offered his own hand then his dad's and Max responded to the game as if he, too, enjoyed it. Over their heads, Ben's gaze met Ms. Nicols's. He mouthed, "Thanks."

She gave one of her smiles again and mouthed, "My pleasure."

And Ben thought she meant it.

Max circled Kyle, straining for a better lick at his hands. His tail swished a pile of leaves, reminding Kyle of the previous game. He leapt into a pile, grabbing an armful of leaves and tossing them. Max's front feet left the ground as tried to catch leaves in his month. Max and Kyle romped through the leaves, both with huge grins on their faces.

Ben and Ms. Nicols watched the two frolic. Ben mused, "Kyle's playing. He's actually playing."

"Yes," Ms. Nicols agreed. "It's lovely to see." Then, she added, "You're doing a good job with him."

Ben turned to her in surprise. She'd given him exactly the opposite opinion last week and he said so.

"I might have been a bit hard on you at first. Sorry. I thought you were another uninvolved parent and these kids really need their mothers and fathers behind them one hundred percent. I was wrong about you, though. You do care."

"Damned right I do. But I have no idea how to do this."

"Who does? Kids don't come with a rule book, especially kids with autism."

Ben let that last bit go. "But you're right. I was an uninvolved father." He told her how he'd only learned of Kyle's existence when the child was two, when Deanna had called asking for money. He remembered cradling the phone in one ear, listening to her, while he used his computer to search for flights to LA to go meet his son. Deanna had heard the tap-tapping through the phone lines and asked what he was doing. In no uncertain terms she told him he was not welcome to visit them in LA. Kyle was just starting to adjust to her boyfriend who had recently moved in. Having one father was all Kyle could cope with now. Meeting Ben would only confuse and upset him.

"I'm ashamed to say that I took Deanna's word for that and did not push a face-to-face meeting. Instead, I just sent money. Some father, huh, Ms. Nicols?"

"It's not what you did then, but what you're doing now that counts. And my name's Melanie."

"Yeah? That suits you. Melanie." They smiled at each other.

Ben reached out and brushed some leaves from Melanie's hair, leaves put there by an exuberant Kyle. Or, maybe they were from Max who was spreading almost as many leaves around as his playmate with two hands. The button on Ben's coat snagged the covered elastic holding Melanie's ponytail, pulling it most of the way out. Her hair tumbled around her face. Ben stared. Her hair was gorgeous and framed a face that was lovely in the sunshine.

She reached to repair her ponytail. Ben impulsively stayed her hand. "Don't. It looks nice like that." Uncertain, Melanie complied.

They watched the boy and dog a few minutes more but gone was that easy camaraderie between the two of them. Ben thought

Kyle showed signs of tiring. Melanie thought he showed signs of getting too wrought up. Time to switch activities, she thought.

But that's as far ahead as her brain thought. The next words out of her mouth surprised even her. "Who wants hot chocolate?"

"Kyle. Kyle wants hot chocolate," Kyle said, referring to himself. "And Max. Max wants hot chocolate."

Ben looked around. He didn't remember seeing a restaurant or a take-out stand around here.

Now Melanie's face was reddened, but not from the sun or wind. "I meant at my place. I don't live far from here and I have hot chocolate." She rushed on, "I didn't mean to impose. Of course you're busy. Don't feel obligated...."

Ben studied her. "What do you say, Kyle? Want to go have hot chocolate with Ms. Nicols and Max?"

"Yeeees!"

"Kind of hard for you to back out now." Ben grinned at Melanie.

Melanie's house was three blocks the other side of the park. Max was now on a leash, walking beside Kyle, while Ben and Melanie brought up the rear. Kyle walked with one fist bunched in Max's ruff; both seemed content. The adults were not quite so peaceful with each other.

"Are you regretting your offer? We can just walk you home then leave if you want. I'll make up an excuse to Kyle." Ben sensed that Melanie wished she had never opened her mouth.

"No, it's not that." Melanie paused, and then being forthright, said what was on her mind. "It's just that we're not friends."

Ben raised an eyebrow at her.

"I don't mean we can't be friends. Well, we can't really. I'm your son's teacher. I have a policy about not dating in the workplace and certainly not a student's parent." Her face was again red.

"A date is usually something I plan. We had no idea we'd run into you at the park. You didn't know either."

"True, but…"

"So, we're just acquaintances being social and sharing a warm drink on a fall day."

By then they were in front of Melanie's house. It was the quintessential white picket fence bungalow, although small. Tiny, in fact.

"How many bedrooms does this place have? Half of one?"

Melanie gave him a mock glare. "Two, if you must know. Or more like one and a half. There's my room then a small room I use as an office for my school stuff."

As soon as the gate was opened and Melanie unsnapped the leash, Max took off, spinning circles in the front yard, running back and forth in front of Kyle, trying to get him to play.

"Is it all right?" Ben asked, but was too late as Kyle tore around the side of the house after the dog. In the fading distance, they could hear the dog's glad bark and Kyle's answering giggle.

"Is Max safe?"

"I'd stake my life on it. And Kyle's," she answered. "Come on in." She turned the key in the lock, then pushed on the door with her shoulder. It didn't budge. She stood back, and then tried again. Ben placed his hand flat on the door above her head and pushed with her. "The front door's a bit tricky," she explained.

Only a few strides took them right through the house to the back door. Melanie unlocked the knob, opened the door and called out to Kyle to come right in when he wanted.

Ben leaned against the kitchen counter as Melanie got out a pot and the ingredients. Soon the kitchen felt cozy with the smell of the warming milk. The place suited Melanie. It was homey but uncluttered, everything in its place. Ben smiled to himself as he thought that at least her hair was not in place.

Melanie caught Ben's frequent glances out the back door window to check on Kyle. She liked that his son was never far from his mind. She suggested, "Why don't we take our mugs and sit outside where we can watch them".

They relaxed on the wide Adirondack chairs. In the lee of the wind with the late afternoon sun shining on them, the weather was just right. So was the company, Ben thought in surprise. Around them, his son and Melanie's dog bounded with endless energy. Ben could not tell which of the two was having the most fun. Periodically Kyle swooped by for a slurp of his hot chocolate then charged off again with Max in pursuit.

As it began to grow chillier, Ben called Kyle over to finish his hot chocolate. Feeling the back of Kyle's hand, Ben thought he was getting a bit cold, so he sat him on his lap and shared his jacket with his son. Kyle snuggled in and drank his cocoa. When he put the cup down, he sank back down into his dad's arms and relaxed. In about a minute he was asleep. Ben gazed at his slumbering son, then remembered where they were.

He started to apologize and to rouse Kyle.

"No, no, he's fine. Just stay there. He's had a big day and looks worn out. Let him recharge his batteries a few minutes."

"Well, if you're sure," Ben told her.

They sat in companionable silence, Max collapsing at their feet and shutting his eyes as well. Ben relaxed, loving the feel of a warm boy in his arms and the sun on his face. It was nice to sit here with his son, a friendly dog and an attractive, pretty amazing woman. The sun was warm and so far it had been a good day.

Melanie watched as Ben drifted off, joining his son and her dog in sleep. What did that say about her company, she wondered? But this did give her an opportunity to study Ben. His face looked softer, younger in sleep. He showed a vulnerable side he'd never allow to sneak out when he was awake.

She'd misjudged him. She chided herself for making snap judgments, but she was not usually wrong. She'd had him pegged as an uncaring suit, a businessman who had little time for anything other than work, and certainly no time for his son. At first she figured his wife had roped him in for some child care time. Then when she learned that he was a single parent, she assumed he was one of those dead beat dads, only now being called to task to take some responsibility for his child. But, take responsibility he had. Oh, there had certainly been some glitches and he still had a lot to learn, but he was trying. You could see the difference in Kyle.

And today, today had been an eye-opener for her. When she spied them across the park, she instantly dismissed them as just people who only resembled Kyle and Ben. The Mr. Wickens she knew would never risk getting his suit rumpled or his clothes dirty by roughhousing with his son. He'd never risk losing his dignity by playing in the leaves with a child. Actually, like a child. But Ben had seemed to be having just as much fun as Kyle and when he recognized her, he didn't stop in embarrassment. Yes, there was more to this Ben Wickens than she had thought.

As she gazed at him, she did not like the direction her thoughts were heading. This was the parent of one of her students, after all. To distract herself, she got up and went into the kitchen. Might as well make herself useful and create a treat for Kyle. Living with a single dad, he might not get many homemade treats. She smiled at her own admittedly chauvinistic thoughts.

"Anyone for peanut-butter cookies?"

Ben came to with a start. Where was he? Oh, shit. Now he remembered. Had he actually fallen asleep on his son's teacher's deck? And what was that heavenly aroma?

Melanie stood at the door, delectable smells drifting over the two snoozing Wickens men.

Kyle woke up. "Cookies," he yelled and just like that he was off Ben's knee and into the open kitchen door.

Ben could hear Melanie instructing him to first wash his hands then have a seat at the table. It took Ben longer to gather his wits, then he followed his son back inside the house. He saw that the table was set for three. A glass of milk was in front of one place setting. A bottle of beer stood by each of the two other plates. Ben smiled. The end to a perfect afternoon.

By the time they walked home, Ben was ready for supper. Unfortunately, with a son to look after, he needed to provide healthy meals. No more calling for pizza delivery and having a cold brew in front of the television. So he got Kyle settled with his building blocks and went to work on supper.

What guy didn't know how to fry a couple steaks or chops? Ben was no different.

He put some water on to boil for pasta and heated the oil in the frying pan.

The phone rang. It was Ellie, Ben's sister. Ben was her go-to person when it came to finances and their family's bakery. Balancing the books was always a issue with that bakery. Ben kept the books for them and the ledgers were in his desk.

Ben sat behind his desk to search for the answer to Ellie's pressing question. Their conversation got involved as they weighed options.

Kyle wandered into the kitchen. He stared, mesmerized by the swirling pattern of smoke rising from the pan on the stove. Moving closer, he poked at the smoke, liking the way his finger dispersed the pattern. He pushed his finger closer to the pan, but drew back sharply when some grease sputtered and burned him.

Watching some more, Kyle noticed a dish towel hanging over the oven door handle. He grabbed the towel and used that to poke at the smoke. The tail of the towel floated close to the gas burner. At first there was just a spark and the edges turned black. Then flames burst onto the edge and rapidly spread up the towel. Kyle watched, fascinated.

In no time, the flames reached his hand. The sensation didn't register for a second, then it did. Kyle screamed! He tried to shake the towel off of his hand, but part of it stuck. Kyle waved the towel, fanning the flames. He dropped the flaming towel into the hot pan of grease. More flames burst forth.

From the den, Ben heard Kyle's screams. Throwing down the phone, he raced to the kitchen. At first he couldn't see his son due to the grayish smoke making swirling patterns in much of the room and covering the stove with a smoke like dense fog.

Ben peered through the smoke frantically and found Kyle. Part of a flaming towel was on his son's hand. Flames erupted on the sleeve of Kyle's shirt. Ben threw the child to the floor, fell with him, smothering the flames with his own body. He used his hands to bat at the flames still on the towel, while trying to grab Kyle's hands and press them between their bodies.

Mindful of his own greater weight, Ben quickly rolled off his son, eyes alert for any further signs of flames on the little boy's clothes. Although Ben could not see any more fire on him, Kyle continued to scream.

Then the condition of the rest of the room penetrated Ben's panic. Flames were rising higher on the stove. Remnants of the dish towel still smoldered. Leaving Kyle momentarily, Ben grabbed a box of salt in one hand, the box of baking powder in the other. He hesitated before throwing either on the fire. Grease, grease, grease. Which did you use for a grease fire? He couldn't remember and couldn't take a chance. He threw both boxes to the ground and pulled the drawer off its runners to the floor in his search for a lid for the pot. Ah, he found it and slammed the lid onto the pot. The hiss of the smoke and grease was now smothered but smoke still billowed out from the edges. Shit! The burner was still on.

There. The fire was out. While the smoke wasn't dying down, at least the amount pouring out was less.

He heard Kyle coughing on the floor behind him. Ben picked up his son, cradling him in his arms and ran to the bathroom to look at the damages.

Kyle's screaming had subsided to whimpers and coughs. Ben tore the remnants of Kyle's shirt away. Miraculously, despite the flames he had seen, the harm to Kyle seemed slight. He must have let go of the towel soon enough, or only the outside parts of the damp towel had burned, the wetter areas shielding the kid from the worst of the flames. Although the sleeve of his shirt was scorched and full of holes, Kyle's arm looked okay. Ben stood Kyle on the vanity and ran his hands over his jeans. They looked fine in the front. He turned him around, careful to balance him with one hand. No, he had not been burned on the back of his legs either. There were no marks at all on Kyle's back and only a slight redness on his arms. The most injured part Ben could see was a burn on Kyle's right index finger.

With his heart still beating a staccato tempo Ben asked Kyle over and over if he was all right, if he hurt anyplace. Kyle didn't reply; Ben had to reassure himself by checking over every inch of Kyle's skin.

Thank god the child was all right. What kind of a father was he to have let such a thing happen to his son? Kyle'd only been with him such a short time and look, he'd almost been killed. Well, not quite killed, but he could have been in just a couple more minutes.

Ben fished under the bathroom sink for first aid supplies. He held Kyle's finger under the cold, running water. At first Kyle yelled and fought him, not heeding Ben's words that this would make him feel better. Slowly it sank in, that his finger was actually hurting less now. Ben instructed Kyle to leave his finger under the water while he sorted out the bandages and burn salve. After gently wrapping the hurt finger loosely in gauze then surgical tape, Ben lifted Kyle off the vanity. He held his son in his arms tightly, apologizing for not paying attention and allowing Kyle to get hurt.

Then his voice rose as he told Kyle to never, ever, touch that stove again. Ben crushed Kyle to him once again and carried him in his arms to the couch, where he sat rocking him.

As Ben's heart rate slowed, the rest of the world started to enter his senses. There was the smell of little boy hair and sweat against his face. He could smell the ointment he'd just applied. In the background was the smell of smoke and singed material. While the smoke had been concentrated in the kitchen, some tendrils had drifted down the hallway and into the living room. The mess in the kitchen and airing the place out would all need to be attended to but for now, Ben just wanted to sit and hold the miracle that was his precious little boy.

What was that? What could he hear? It was kind of tinny and sounded far away. Ben did not want any more surprises tonight so he set Kyle down to go investigate.

The sound got louder as he went down the hall. He paused in the doorway to his den. Yes, he could hear it louder in here. It sounded like a voice. He walked to his desk and looked underneath. There on the floor was his cordless phone and the noise was coming from it. He put it to his ear and listened.

"Mom?" he asked.

He had to move the phone away from his ear when she screeched her frantic reply. This didn't make sense. Before the fire, Ben had been on the phone with his little sister. He didn't think he'd hung up but couldn't remember what he'd done in his panic when he heard Kyle's scream.

Gradually his mother's words lowered in volume and stridency, making them easier to understand. Yes, Ben had been on the phone with his sister. Through the phone Ellie had heard Kyle's screams then a thud. That would have been when Ben threw the phone. Ellie had remained on the phone, frantically calling to Ben to learn what was happening. Did he need help? Was he all right? Why was there a child screaming in the background?

Ellie had held on for several minutes. She'd yelled for her mother to come hold that phone while she scrambled for her cell to call Ben's cell. No answer. Desperate, not knowing if they should call the police or 911, Ellie paced with the phone in her hand. The screams subsided. Straining to hear, Ellie thought she could hear her brother's voice low in the distance but not yelling. So maybe it wasn't a 9-1-1 situation.

But Ben had always been there for Ellie and it was not often he needed something from her. So, while their mother stayed on the line, calling out to Ben to return to the phone, Ellie grabbed her jacket and car keys. She'd drive over to Ben's to check it out, while their mother remained on the phone, hoping to be able to talk to Ben.

"Sorry, mom, sorry to have worried you. We're all right," Ben explained. "There was a little fire, a grease fire on the stove, but it's under control now."

"What was all that screaming Ellie said she heard? She thought it sounded like a child"

Ben sighed. This was so not the way he wanted to break the news about Kyle to his parents.

"It was a child. A little boy. His name is Kyle, and he's staying with me."

There was silence on his mother's end of the phone. What the hell, he might as well just plunge in now.

"He's my son, mom. I know this will come as a shock to you. He's been with me this past couple weeks. I wanted to give him time to get used to being here before I introduced him to the rest of my family." Silence. "Mom? Mom, are you there? Are you all right?

"Look, it's a long story. I was going to tell you this week anyway. I can't get into it right now. I have to go check on Kyle. I'll call you later and tell you everything. Okay?"

"You'd better. You have a lot of explaining to do, young man."

Ben grinned despite the situation. Those were the exact words his mother had used on him when he was growing up and found himself in trouble. This time, she was right, oh so right. He really did have a lot of explaining to do.

CHAPTER 7

The bell rang. Ah, that had to be Ellie. Much as Ben loved his sister, he so did not want to have to deal with her or anyone for that matter, right now. He'd had enough for the day, enough fun and enough sun and enough drama. Cripes. He's had more crises in the past week since Kyle had come into his life than for years put together. But, today's fire was not Kyle's fault. It was Ben's responsibility as a dad to look after his son. He'd failed. Maybe Kyle would be better off back home with his mother.

Ben's gut clenched at the thought. He'd begun by accepting Kyle as his responsibility. But somehow, sometime, it had grown to be much more than that. The kid had gotten under his skin and as much as his days had been thrown into a spin, he could hardly imagine life now without Kyle in it.

Delaying it would not make this any easier. From the repeated and ferocious ringing of the doorbell, Ellie was not going to wait much longer. As that thought left his brain and his foot took that first step towards the door, that bell was joined by a pounding fist and a kicking foot. His sister could be a feisty thing and had been since she could barely toddle around chasing after her big brothers.

Kyle, who had calmed after the excitement, again tensed. This pounding was the last straw. Ben now knew the signs of an incoming storm. He pressed firmly on both of Kyle's shoulders and crouched down to his level. Over his shoulder, he yelled towards the door. "Hang on a sec, El. I'm coming. We're all right."

"Ben?" The muffled voice came through the heavy door. "Ben, are you all right? Who's we?"

"Kyle, it's your aunt Ellie come to visit us. She wants to know that we're not hurt from the fire. It'll be all right."

Still pressing firmly, he led the boy toward the door and held him to his side as he opened the door. Knowing his sister, he made sure Kyle was safely out of the way of the swinging door.

On cue, Ellie burst in. She looked like she might have been in some sort of crisis herself. Her wavy black hair was tousled, either from a wind storm or from obsessively running her fingers through it. Her pale blue eyes were wild as they scanned Ben from head to toe. Her hands grabbed at him.

"You're all right? You're OK?" she demanded.

"We're fine. The place smells a bit badly and there's cleaning to be done, but we're all right."

"We?" Ellie's eyes drifted to the little boy half hidden by Ben's legs. Kyle's face peeked out but his eyes were on her shoes.

And well they might be, thought Ben. Ellie must have been relaxing at home because she still had on her plush, grey hippopotamus slippers - a gag Christmas gift from their youngest brother many years ago. Although they looked decidedly the worse for wear, she forsook all other footwear when lounging at home. In her haste to check on Ben's situation she had obviously given no thought to her appearance. Ben smiled. Ellie really was a good kid and not at all the girly-girl type their dad believed.

"Come in, El. Have a seat. There's quite a bit to tell you."

"I'm not budging an inch until I learn who this is and what's going on here."

Ben's shoulders dropped and he let out a breath. In this mood, there was no point in arguing with Ellie. He'd tried in the past and it never worked.

"Ellie, I'd like you to meet your nephew, Kyle. Kyle Wickens." He squatted beside Kyle, lifting the child onto his one knee. "Kyle, this is your aunt Ellie. She's my sister," he added, then wondered if a five year old, only child had such a concept.

Kyle remained silent, his eyes on those slippers.

Ellie, bless her heart, lowered her volume and the stridency. She, too, crouched down, her face almost level with Kyle's. "Hi," she said. "I'm very pleased to meet you. I'm El." She put out her hand.

"Kyle, can you shake hands with Aunt Ellie?" Ben said.

No response. Ben repeated his words, careful to use the exact phrasing. Ellie raised her eyes to Ben's and he warned her with a look. Thankfully, Ellie caught on and just waited quietly. In his head, Ben counted to ten, then to fifteen, as Ms. Nicols - no, Melanie, he remembered with a smile - had instructed him to do. It was this wait time thing and something to do with auditory processing being slower in kids with autism. Autism. How was he going to explain that one to his sister? His sister, hell, she was going to be the easy one. Wait till he tried to tell his father, the guy who had never understood even one of his three children. Nor, had he put much effort into that, Ben reflected.

"Will you shake hands with me, Kyle?" Ellie asked, mimicking Ben's words, bless her.

"Handshake, hug or high five," Kyle repeated. Ellie looked quizzically at Ben.

"That's what his teacher asks each kid as they leave her room at the end of the day. They all get the choice," Ben explained.

"Ah, makes sense," Ellie said, as if this was all part of normal life. For Ben, it sure wasn't. Or had been, he reminded himself.

"Which should we do, Kyle? A handshake, hug or high five?" Ellie asked then waited.

Without raising his eyes to hers, Kyle replied, "Hug." He moved off Ben's knee and put his arms around Ellie's neck. She squeezed him back, tightly. Her eyes meeting Ben's were moist.

Ben was as proud of his son as if he had taught Kyle these social graces himself.

Kyle pulled away, his eyes returning to Ellie's feet. He said, "Dora the Explorer. Diego's Hippo Adventure." While Ben had thought he'd learned more this week than he had ever wanted to know about Dora, this stuff about a Diego and some hippo was new to him. However, Ellie didn't seem in the dark.

"Ah, so you know about Dora, too. Do you have a book about Diego and the hippo? Or the video?" she asked Kyle. Kyle didn't answer but turned and headed down the hall towards the living room. Ellie followed, her nose like a dog sniffing the air, giving Ben a look over her shoulder. It was a WTF kind of look.

Ben surveyed the mess in the kitchen. This was going to take a looong time to fix. He started by opening the window and turning on the fan over the stove. Grabbed a pot holder and tossed the ruined frying pan and remnants of the towel into the sink. He needn't have bothered with the pot holder and the pan was barely warm now. But as it hit the sink, the bottom of the pan separated from the sides. Sheesh, it must have gotten hot. When he thought of what could have happened... How could he have left a pan of oil heating on the stove? And, most important, how could he have forgotten he was no longer just fending for himself but had a child to consider?

The child. Cripes. Once again, Kyle had slipped his mind. It was only for a few moments, but look what could happen in just minutes. The nightmare wreck of his kitchen reminded him. Ben went to open the door to the condo hallway, thinking to air the place out still more. When he opened the door, faint smoky patterns drifted by him into the hallway. As he watched the smoke curl, he hastily shut the door. What if the wafting smoke set off the building smoke detectors? Or worse, the sprinkler system? No telling what damage that would do.

Smoke detectors. Why hadn't his gone off? With the amount of smoke, they certainly should have. There was one in his hall, right outside the kitchen door, wasn't there? Yep. Oh. Then, Ben remembered. One night, months ago, the stupid thing had started beeping in the night, low on batteries. While he had an assortment of batteries in a drawer, none were the right size. To stop the infernal thing from beeping he had unhooked the inside wires, then forgotten all about it. First thing in the morning he was replacing the batteries in every smoke detector. And, he was buying two fire extinguishers - one for the kitchen and one to go beside the fireplace.

What else did parents do? The fire department might have suggestions on their website. And, hadn't he seen some advertisement on television about having a safety plan, an evacuation drill that you practiced with your kids. He'd need to get on that. Maybe Melanie knew about this stuff; she seemed to know everything there was to know about kids. There really was a lot to this parenting stuff.

Parenting. He'd done it again, forgotten about Kyle for minutes more. At least there were no screams. Instead, there was the low murmur of voices, or at least one voice - Ellie's.

In the den, Ellie sat on the couch, with an opened book in her lap. Another one of Kyle's endless Dora books. That chick Dora really got around, Ben thought. There was a story or video about her and her friends in almost every part of the world, or so Ben had experienced so far from reading and watching with Kyle.

As Ellie read aloud with Kyle beside her, Ben watched Kyle edge closer. Soon, there was no space between their bodies. Ellie, still reading, glanced at Kyle out of the corner of her eye. She paused, asking him to point to something in the picture. As he did, she put her arm around him, snuggling him close. Rather than pulling away or howling as he had the first time Ben tried to tentatively touch Kyle that way, he relaxed against his aunt, naming the objects in the background of the picture.

It had taken days for Kyle to let him touch him, Ben thought with chagrin, and within a half hour of meeting Ellie, he allowed her touch. Here Ben thought he and his son had bonded over the course of this past week, when Ellie had accomplished as much as he in just a fraction of the time.

What would Ms. Nicols - Melanie - say about that? It was nice to think of her now as Melanie and perhaps not just Melanie, his son's teacher but possibly, Melanie a friend. He had certainly come to trust her advice on Kyle.

Okay. She said not to take things personally, especially with kids with autism. The child's reactions might have nothing to do with you, she had said. Instead, it might be more to do with something going on inside him, some sensory sensitivities, some reaction to the environment, fatigue or overload.

Look at how Ellie held him. Firmly. She seemed to know instinctively how Kyle liked to be held, while Ben had struggled to treat the kid like spun glass. His initial touches had been tentative and light, in his efforts to be gentle and not startle this little man. Melanie had explained that to some kids light, feathery touches on their skin were akin to finger nails on a blackboard for other people. The light touch might send his nerve endings jangling, while a firmer touch could be calming. In fact, she'd said to press much harder than you would think you would have to for a child of that age.

That's why she used a weighted blanket in the classroom when kids were upset. That's why they had bean bag chairs that kids could sink into. That's why they had weighted lap pillows or tube "snakes" to drape around their shoulders and big cushions to crawl under. Weight and pressure could have a soothing effect. Once Ben learned to use pressure, rather than a light touch, his son actually gravitated to him, rather than shied away from his touch. Much more gratifying to a new father.

It was also gratifying to see his son so cozy with his aunt. Ah, families. Somehow, cozying up brought an image of Melanie. He'd certainly never be that close to her, but what might it be like?

"Everything okay here?" It certainly looked that way to Ben, but it didn't hurt to check.

"Why don't you do something about your disaster zone? We're fine," said Ellie.

"We're fine," echoed Kyle. He gave his dad a smile. God that kid could get to him, Ben thought.

Ben grabbed some garbage bags and tackled the worst of the kitchen. He went through two sponges, trying to scour the stove and sink. The smell still lingered. Next, he mopped the floor and took the garbage to the trash can out back. Still, there was the smell of smoke. On television ads, some woman would come in and spray some stuff in the air and everyone would sniff and smile. Somehow, Ben thought it would take more than that to solve this problem.

He went around the condo opening all the windows, despite the chill of the evening air. He didn't want Kyle getting cold, so he lit the fireplace in the den, then threw a heavy comforter over both his son and his sister. They snuggled in.

"That was supposed to be dinner and I don't fancy trying to cook anything else in that room now. Would you be all right with Kyle if I ran out for some pizza?"

"We're fine. Go ahead. Make my side double cheese, don't forget. And no anchovies," Ellie said.

A little head peaked out from under the blanket. "No anchovies!" Ellie and Ben laughed, both doubting that the kid had any idea what an anchovy even was. But, he was certainly taking to his new aunt, and Ben would take any words his son uttered. Was it his imagination, or was Kyle actually speaking more?

The aroma of pizza preceded Ben into the condo. He set the extra-large pizza box on the coffee table in front of his two favorite people. Next he brought out three plates and tore a bunch of paper towels off the kitchen rolls for napkins. He brought extras, having experience now with the way a young boy eats.

Ben served while Ellie wrapped up what must be her fourth book, judging from the stack beside Kyle. He gave Kyle a plate with a large slice. He handed Ellie a piece from the double cheese, no meat or veggies side. Kyle stiffened when he looked at his plate. Ben, knowing the signs asked, "What is it bud? Don't you like pizza?" Kyle held the plate out at arm's length and looked ready to throw it. "What, what's wrong?" Ben said.

"He doesn't like it, there's something about it he doesn't like," said Ellie. "While you were gone, we talked about pizza and I think he was looking forward to it."

"Quick, grab it," she said, sensing Kyle was about to throw or thrust the plate away from him. Ben complied.

Kyle whimpered. "What's wrong?" Ben repeated. "What do you want?"

"It's touching. No, no, no!" came from Kyle.

Ben and Ellie looked at each other. What's touching? He and Ellie were touching and had been for some time now. What was bugging the kid?

Kyle reached for Ellie's plate and took it from her hands. He grabbed her pizza slice and started eating.

"Hey," his father yelled. "Kyle, that's rude. Put that back."

Kyle looked like he was about to cry, but gave Ellie back her plate. He just sat there, staring at the pizza box.

Ellie studied Kyle, her plate and the pizza. Then it hit her. "Ben, don't you remember Samuel when he was little? Remember what a picky eater he was? He hated the foods on his plate to touch each other. Mom had that little kid's divided plate that he used for years so it would keep the different foods separate. Maybe Kyle doesn't like his things touching either."

Maybe Ellie was on to something. Ben remembered words, "Don't take it personally. Odds are, it's not about you." Okay, if he looked at it like that, maybe Kyle was not just being rude. Ben studied Kyle's plate and Ellie's. Ellie's looked bland, all one color with just melted cheese on her crust. The pizza slices on Ben and

Kyle's plates were colorful with a variety of meat and vegetables poking out from the cheese. It was worth a try.

"Kyle, do you like this one better?" Ben pointed at the all-cheese side of the pizza pie. Kyle just looked at the cheese side.

Ben placed Kyle's slice onto his own plate then put a cheese only slice onto Kyle's plate. His son rewarded him with a smile and reached for the plate. Why he hadn't just said something, Ben wondered. He met Ellie's gaze and read the question in them. "Later," he mouthed.

Kyle's eyes drooped by the end of the meal. Ellie asked if Kyle usually had a bath before bed. When Ben nodded, she became almost shy, unusual for her. She asked, "Would it be all right if I gave him his bath and put him to bed?" At Ben's nod, she turned to Kyle. He stood up and held out his hand to her.

When Ben checked in on them a while later, they were both making motor noises with their mouths as they drove bars of soap through the water. Folding his arms and leaning against the door jamb, Ben asked Ellie, "What made you give him a bath instead of a shower?"

Ellie looked at him like he was a moron. Probably only because of Kyle's presence did she not tell him so. "Ben, he's a little kid. What did you think? How old were you when you switched from baths to showers? Don't you even remember being a little boy?"

Come to think of it, she was right. They had always had baths when they were children. It was only in his teen years that Ben could remember showering. Just one more example of why he wouldn't be getting any Father of the Year award.

After Ellie read Kyle yet one more Dora the Explorer book and they both tucked him into bed, then Ben and Ellie each nursed bottles of stout in front of the fire.

"So, come on, big brother. Give. I want all the details." Ellie continued, "But first, when are you gonna buy that kid a bed? Just how long are you going to have him sleep on the couch in your office?"

Ben had actually forgotten that that might be a problem. Kyle's first night with him, it had seemed like a huge problem. He'd had no idea where to put the kid, until he spied the fold-out couch in the den.

Ben's condo had two bedrooms. Since he lived alone, he'd turned the smaller room into a den. His desk took up most of the middle of the room, one wall was solid book case and a leather fold-out couch took up another wall. When it was folded out for Kyle at night, there was barely room to get between the desk and the wall. Kyle's suitcase was open in another corner of the room, with clothes and toys and books strewn over almost every square inch of visible floor space. Ben had been meaning to clean it up, but had gotten distracted numerous times. It was a daunting task, because just where was he going to put things? His desk drawers were full. The book shelves were filled and there wasn't room for a dresser in the room.

Ellie wasn't finished. "And, did you watch how close Kyle's head came to the corner of this coffee table? Several times, in fact, when he was sitting on the floor." Ben looked at the offending table. It had come with the place when he hired a decorator to furnish it for him. The half inch sheet of beveled glass sat on a molded ceramic base, sculpted to resemble something or other. Ben had never figured out just what. It was a table to put stuff on and doubled as a foot rest when he watched television. Looking closely now, he noticed the dozens and dozens of little finger prints all over the glass surface. He guessed that Millie had not been here for a few days. She must be the one wiping and polishing its surface.

Was that fair to Millie? Perhaps this wasn't the most kid-friendly sort of table. Looking closer, neither was the white Berber carpet its base sat on, nor the white leather sofa. Actually, when did this room get so white? Ben knew it had been the same since he moved it, and had never given his decor any thought. Who in their right mind wants to live in an all-white room? And who was expected to keep it clean? Wouldn't something dirt-colored be more practical?

Ellie watched him steadily as these thoughts flittered through his mind. She would wait no longer for her answers, so Ben plunged in.

He told her how he and Deanna had dated years ago, but parted amicably when she accepted a job offer in California. He'd not heard from her again until she called one night, upset. Honestly, when she identified herself as Deanna, it had taken a second for him to place her. Ellie's face mirrored Ben's initial shock when Deanna told him he had a son.

"Did you question if it really was your kid?" Ellie asked.

Ben paused and looked at her. If Deanna said he had fathered the child, he had no reason to doubt her. The timing fit. Roughly. Ben dismissed that thought from his mind.

"So, if she hadn't needed money, would you ever have known you had a kid?" Ellie said.

"I'm not sure. I'd like to think she'd have let me know, but she didn't when she was pregnant and she didn't for Kyle's first two years of life. God, am I that unapproachable of a bastard?"

"No. You said that she said she wanted a child. You were likely an acceptable sperm donor."

Ben just looked at her.

"You may be my big brother, but I'm not blind. I've seen women look at you. Don't let it go to your head, but you are good looking. And, at least most of the time, you're an okay guy."

"Thanks. At least I think."

Ellie made carry on motions with her index finger.

Ben continued, telling her the reason Deanna called was that she needed money. Ellie rolled her eyes. Ben felt the need to defend Deanna. After all, she had never asked him for anything for the previous three years, when she certainly could have. She'd gone through the whole pregnancy and baby thing without any help at all from him, the father, the one who should have shouldered the responsibility.

There was more to it, he told her. Kyle had not been an easy child and by age two he wasn't talking. Deanna had taken him to doctors and therapists for help and to figure out what was wrong. They gave Kyle a diagnosis. Autism.

Ben watched his sister. She didn't look shocked or surprised. Was he the only one who didn't know about autism? She nodded at him to continue.

Kyle needed treatment. The therapists Deanna went to told her that the only proven treatment for autism was something called Applied Behavior Analysis or ABA for short.

"Okay, so what's the problem?" Ellie asked.

Money, he explained. The treatment was expensive.

"Well, you have insurance. She probably has insurance through her job as well."

It was not that easy, Ben told her. Insurance would only cover a part of it and the rest had to be dredged up by the families.

"Just how much are we talking?" Ellie asked.

It was hard to give an exact figure, depending on how the child responded, but it usually worked out to about sixty thousand a year.

"Dollars?" Ellie's eyebrows rose.

Ben nodded. A year. It cost so much because the treatment was individual and required a trained therapist.

"Hokey. That therapist must be raking it in for a few hours office visit a week."

Ben shook his head this time. "There aren't office visits. The therapy is done in the home and it takes up to eight hours a day, five days a week. Then on the weekend and evenings, the parents are supposed to carry on using the same methods."

Ellie was incredulous. "That's forty hours a week, the same as an adult works. When's the kid supposed to play? To nap? To just be a kid?"

Deanna had been told that this was necessary if she wanted to have a good outcome for Kyle's life. If he had this therapy, early intervention, they called it, then Kyle would be cured and ready for regular education when he hit school age.

"How did she come up with the money for it?" Ellie queried. Then, before Ben could reply, she said, "You. Of course. That's just like something you would do. No wonder you've been putting in the hours you do these last few years."

They sat in silence a minute. Ellie, not usually tactful with him, asked, rather hesitantly, "But, does he seem cured to you?"

Exactly Ben's thoughts. And those of Melanie and even the school principal had seemed to recognize autism in Kyle within just a few minutes of meeting him.

"No." His word hung in the air.

"So that's why he doesn't talk much." She waited a few moments. "But I wonder what he was like before? Maybe he'd be a lot worse if he had not had that ABA. Who knows?"

After a few minutes, Ellie apologized. "Sorry for ragging on you about this condo and Kyle's bed. You have bigger worries at the moment."

Ellie leaned forward to grab a remote off the coffee table. She looked at the three remotes laying there, each with more buttons than any one of hers. "Which one turns on the TV?" she asked. "Sheesh. What does anyone want with all these buttons?"

Ben reached for the right one and turned on the news. It was a family tradition to watch the eleven o'clock newscast.

"That's another thing. Kyle. That kid is amazing," he told his sister.

She grinned at him. "I see you're already a doting dad. Nice to see, bro.

94

Ben turned a bit red and carried on. "That first night I got hardly any sleep. Sheesh, this was just dumped on me. I knew nothing about being a father. So, I guess I slept in a bit the next morning and heard noise in the place. I thought someone had broken in.

"I grabbed my pants and went down the hall, trying to be silent until I saw what was up. There was Kyle, sitting beside the pointed end of that coffee table, watching TV. At least at first I thought it was a television show but it turns out he was watching a DVD - one of his DVDs. A Dora one." His sister gave a knowing grin.

Ben continued. "You know how I am about my electronics equipment."

"Boy, do I ever. You chased me all the way down the block once when we were kids when I'd touched your precious stereo system. And, you've only gotten worse over the years."

"Yeah, well, this stuff's expensive and I put a lot of time into getting exactly the right components.

"Just now you had trouble with the remotes and couldn't even turn the TV on. Would you be able to load and play a DVD? No, I know you wouldn't. I'm not sure most people would, if they weren't familiar with my system.

"I had certainly not shown Kyle how to do this. In fact, I had told him not to touch anything along this wall." Ben pointed to his elaborate shelving system of electronic components. "But here he was. He's five years old, had woken up in a strange place and instead of crying, coming to get me, howling or any other kid thing, he came in here, figured it out and was watching his movie. Yet, he can hardly talk. The kid's a strange mixture of can and can't do things."

"From what I gather, that's autism," Ellie said.

"How would you know that?"

"Because I'm from this planet, you dork? Don't you listen to the news? Read? You hear about autism all over the place nowadays. I think Time Magazine had named Temple Grandin one of the one hundred most influential people of our times."

"Temple who?"

"Oh Ben, you are clueless sometimes. Temple Grandin. She's probably the most famous person with autism. She's a prof at Colorado U, world famous for her innovative cattle handling systems, plus she lectures and has written books on autism. She has autism."

"She has autism and she can do all that?"

"Ben, get with it. There are all kinds of people with autism. Silicon Valley is full of them. Some people with autism need full care all their lives, others are independent."

"So, maybe there's hope for Kyle?"

"Jeez, Ben. You obviously have a lot to learn."

"Thanks for that reminder, little sister." He grabbed for her foot, long years of practice reminding him how much she hated having her feet tickled.

With three brothers, Ellie was adept at avoiding their torments. She rescued her foot then made herself comfortable, snuggling in with the comforter from the arm of the couch.

"It's late and the bakery's closed tomorrow," she told him. "I think I might just crash here for the night, if you don't mind."

"Even though you're a brat, you're welcome to my bed and I can take the couch."

"Thanks, but I'm comfy right here. You're white couch might be impractical, but it's just made to sink into."

That returned Ben's thoughts to the impracticality of this condo for a family, even a family of two. "I wish Kyle could live in the kind of place we had growing up. He needs more room and a yard and an actual neighborhood."

"Well, why don't you move?"

"This place is so handy to my work, just two floors above the office. It was fine when there was just me. But, you're right. The kid can't grow up with no space of his own, living out of a suitcase and crashing on my spare couch."

"I thought you were saving up for a house deposit."

"I was, but I had to give all that to Deanna for Kyle's therapy. I also had to start a college fund for him when I heard I had a kid."

"But you rake in a ton of money. You're always working; you put in more hours in a week than anyone else I know."

"*Did* put in more hours. That's had to stop now that I have Kyle. Who's going to look after him while I work, and I think I need to spend some time with him. Jeez, I'm just getting to know my son after missing the first five years of his life."

Ellie looked at him, mulling over these problems. She dreaded that she was about to add to them.

Ben continued, "I've got a bit of the problem cased now. Remember Millie? The woman who comes in twice a week to clean and cook?"

Ellie nodded.

"Well, she's agreed to give up her other cleaning jobs and work just for me. She'll be here every day until 6:30 when I get home from work. And, she'll pick Kyle up from school, which solves a real problem for me."

"Out with it, El. What's bugging you?" He knew her too well.

"I hate to add to your problems," she said.

"Out with it."

"Okay. I know you have a lot on your plate, but it's the usual. Money and the bakery."

No surprise there, thought Ben. "Anything special this time?"

"No, just dad and everything. We won't be able to make payroll again this month." This was not new although it didn't happen every month, usually just when the bakery's quarterly mortgage payments were due.

The bakery was, in the parents' words, a family business. The trouble was, the majority of the family had nothing to do with it and, more importantly, wanted nothing to do with it. Sure, they'd all worked there as kids - it had been expected. But of all four children in the Wickens family, only one had an actual interest in the bakery - Ellie.

But, of all four kids in the Wickens family, only one was deemed unacceptable by their father to take over the bakery from him - Ellie. And the reason? Because she was female.

Yes in this day and age, there were still a few chauvinists around. Their father was at the head of that list. Sure, Ellie was good enough to work in the bakery, but to run it? Impossible, their father said. Forget the inhuman hours that Ellie put in. Forget the fact that she virtually ran the place.

Well, the last fact wasn't exactly forgotten; it had never been recognized by their father. For some reason, he believed that he still ran the bakery when everyone else knew differently. In a way though, you could see how their dad could have the wrong take. He still went into the bakery some days. He still threw in supply orders. He still gave orders to the staff.

The problem was that all these things he did harmed the bakery. Truly. He still lived back the way things were twenty years ago. If he saw the invoice of an incoming shipment, he'd be aghast at the prices and refuse to accept the order. Then the bakery not only lost the product but had to pay restocking fees.

He'd pop in, look at the shelves and order new supplies, not considering that Ellie might have done this just that morning. When customers asked for a latte or espresso, he'd tell them that they served coffee, just plain coffee and refused to use the bistro machines. Although the bakery ran smoothly on the days he was absent, he would still come in and give the staff orders that conflicted with their usual, efficient way of doing things.

There was no talking to the senior Mr. Wickens about these things. He refused to acknowledge Ellie's role in managing the bakery. The only way he would discuss the running of the bakery was if one of his sons agreed to take over. His sons, not his daughter.

The oldest son had fled to New York. Their father still held out faint hope that Jonathan might uproot his children from school, his wife from her law practice and himself from his job to return to take over the bakery. Since he was a chef, he was already in the food business. Right, their dad reasoned. It all fit. Everyone but their father knew this would never happen. Jonathan had even used words about hell and freezing over the last time he was asked.

Their youngest brother, Samuel, had joined the armed forces to escape their father and the bakery. Of all of them, he had hated the most the hours he'd slaved over making dough and waiting tables. He craved a life of outdoors and action and physical activity.

Then there was Ben. Since he was the only son remaining in the city, their father made it clear that it was now up to him. He said it was Ben's responsibility to take over and to provide for his parents in their old age. Rather than taking up the reins and apprenticing (read slave labor) with their father right after high school, Ben had left for college. But, his choice of major won grudging approval from their father. After all, accounting skills were needed in the bakery, just like any other business.

But Ben had absolutely no interest in the bakery. Instead, over time, he'd started his own accounting firm. Perhaps his early work training in the bakery contributed to his overzealous work ethic, but the long hours had paid off and his accounting firm was thriving. Not that it didn't require constant care and attention on his part, but it was doing well.

So well, in fact, that Ben had propped up the bakery for years. Like many small businesses, it struggled. Under Ellie's guidance, it had limped into the twenty-first century. But whenever their father spied any hint of this change and progress, he'd in no uncertain terms stomp on it. This back and forth cost money in terms of waste and staff. Staff would quit, unclear who their orders should come from. They'd get used to doing things one way, and then Mr. Wickens would pop in and change it all. In the past year, they'd lost two baristas, both fired by Mr. Wickens as needless frivolities. The customers who had come to look forward to the creations served up by these people stopped dropping by. When Ellie introduced low-fat alternatives and soy milk, her father threw out the stores, and ran the products down vocally in front of both staff and customers.

Maybe the bakery could have weathered these storms. Maybe. But the worst hammer that hit their books was the mortgage payments. The second mortgage payments to be exact.

Their parents had purchased the bakery thirty-five years ago. By every estimate that Ben and Ellie could guess at, the bakery property should have been paid off ten years ago at the latest. But, it wasn't and five years ago, their father had taken out a second mortgage on the property.

No one had any idea why or where the money went. No one, that is, except their father and he refused to say. The bakery was his business, he told them and since Ben wouldn't take it over, then the finances were none of his business. And Ellie, well, their father just discounted her entirely. They'd asked their mother numerous times, but she seemed to know no more than her children did about the financial end. Her husband had always handled the money in the family, as fitting a man's role, she told them.

But the quarterly payments for this second mortgage were killing Ellie and the business. Fearing that they'd lose the place, Ellie made these payments above all other bills. But that left a gaping hole every three months for staff salaries and often for suppliers as well.

Step in, Ben. Yes, he had, out of obligation to his sister and to his parents. After all, he was making all right money and what did he have to spend it on? True, he wanted a house - a house with a yard and in a neighborhood where people actually knew each other. As a kid he'd hated when it was his turn cutting the grass but now at the ripe age of thirty-three, owning grass that needed cutting had appeal.

But, his house down payment savings account was now barren, given to Deanna for Kyle's ABA treatment. He didn't resent that, not one bit. For the past few years when he needed to come up with extra cash for the bakery, he'd simply worked longer hours and taken on more clients. Now, his ability to do that was seriously impeded. He had Kyle to look after and needed to spend time with him.

Ben vowed not to be the kind of dad his father had been to him. There was never time for his kids - looking after children was women's work. Never once could Ben remember his father coming to a Little League game or a school play or graduation. Always, the bakery came first.

When he was not at the bakery, their father was home in front on the television with a drink in his hand. When their dad was home, everyone else in the house tiptoed around. They could not disturb their father and that included trying to talk to him. Often the kids would see their dad passed out in his recliner when they went to bed at night and rise in the morning to see him still there, snoring, with unwashed, unpleasant odors emanating from the chair. No one else ever sat in that chair, partly because it was their father's place and partly because no one else wanted to go anywhere near that grubby fabric.

The unwashed part and the hangover/ drunken part had then and still did cause the bakery staff turnover. He was not a pleasant man to work for. Maybe he had been at one time, but not as long as either Ellie or Ben could remember. When they asked their older brother, Jonathan, he replied, "Why do you think he's there and I'm all the way up here in New York?"

Ellie was desperate to save the bakery. Without her constant effort and running interference every time their father showed up, they would have lost the place to foreclosure several years ago.

Even Ben's infusion of cash would not have saved the place from mismanagement.

Ellie had a plan, one she pleaded with Ben to accept. But, he wouldn't. While he didn't mind handing over money without their father's knowledge, he refused to be underhanded enough to go along with her plan.

What Ellie wanted was for Ben to take over the business. This was exactly what their father wanted. Except, in Ellie's mind, Ben would head it in name only. He could leave all the day-to-day work and management to Ellie and their father would never have to know. In Ellie's mind, this was the only way she was ever going to get the bakery and make all the changes that needed to be done.

But, to Ben's mind, this was dishonest and deceitful and he refused to lie to their parents in that way. He was willing to argue all he could with their father to get him to change his mind and pass on the business to Ellie. He'd back his sister all the way. But he would not lie and pretend that he was the owner. They'd been back and forth on this so often each knew the other's arguments by heart, but Ben would not budge. His hope was that their father would be forced to come to his senses and he worked on their mother, trying to get her to help out.

In the meantime, it fell on Ben's shoulders to come up with the money to keep the damn bakery afloat.

"What do you need, El, and when?" he asked her.

"I'm three thousand and a bit short next week's payroll and delivery bills."

Ben tried not to let Ellie see him wince. At one time that would not have been impossibility. He could have written a check for that amount from his savings, then replaced that money by doing a couple extra contracts that month. But now, his savings were no longer flush. Any spare funds he had would now go to the extra money he would be paying Millie to come in every day and be with Kyle, money well spent.

But what to do? In the past, he'd simply spend every night working. He was home alone, so it was no problem. But now he had to spend those evenings with his little son and he wanted to, he really did.

Kyle went to bed ideally by eight o'clock so that should give Ben time to get more work done then, but cripes, it certainly had not worked out that way so far. He had no idea how other parents did it, but by the time he had Kyle in bed, tidied up the place a little and prepared Kyle's lunch to take to school, he was whipped. Working twelve hour days at his accounting firm was a piece of cake compared to spending less than half that much time with one little boy. And to think, some people actually had twins.

CHAPTER 8

He studied the chess board and moved his rook to cover his castle. At first he thought he'd have purposely let his son win these games, because it would hardly be fair to trounce a five year old time after time. But the more they played, the more Ben had to actually think to keep up. His kid was no slouch at chess. Ben could never have imagined that someone so young could be so skilled at this game.

Sunday at home. Ben often took half of Sunday off to just relax or be with his parents and sister, although those latter two things rarely went together – relax and his family. But for today, Ben would not think about those things, but focus just on his own, new family of two.

Waiting between moves gave Ben time to think and sip his coffee. They'd come a ways these past weeks, the two of them. Calling them a unit would be stretching things, but they were on their way to neutral ground and some level of understanding. He thought they'd each given in, just a little. Well, a lot on Ben's part, he reflected but even a little was a lot for a kid with autism, he realized.

Now that Ben had read some more, yeah, his son did seem to have autism. Some of the stuff he read on the internet was downright terrifying – parents in physical battles with their grown autistic children, violence, fear, tears, frustration. But then you read the other stories of kids with autism who were in college, or adults with jobs and families. How could you ever predict which of these outcomes would be Kyle's? Ben squared his shoulders. He knew which were in line for Kyle. Kyle would make it. He would be successful and hopefully independent. And if not, then he'd still have his dad in his corner.

There was this pat, pat, pat on his knee. Ben looked. Yep, his king was cornered. Yet again. He looked more closely and could discern no viable move. A look at his son confirmed his fears. The kid had got him yet again.

Ben grabbed him under the arms for a tickle. Kyle's giggles were music to his ears. It was getting near lunch time, so he picked him up and perched him on his shoulder to head into the kitchen. Instantly Kyle's sounds of glee turned to terror. He clutched at his father's hair, clinging to life.

"Whoa, whoa, little man. Easy. Easy. You're safe." Kyle's cries did not diminish. Ben couldn't set him down because of Kyle's grip on his hair. It was making his eyes water. "Kyle, it's all right. I've got you. I won't let you fall." In desperation, he sat himself back onto the couch, rolled to his side to put Kyle there as well. Inadvertently, he partly rolled on Kyle. As he pressed the little boy into the cushions, Kyle's cries notched down some decibels and the grip on Ben's hair lessened. Ben started to roll off the child, fearful of crushing him. As his weight shifted, Kyle's grip tightened and his cries rose again. Ben lowered himself back onto Kyle and again, the cries became less strident. Ben remained that way for several minutes, feeling the tension leave Kyle's body. They remained pressed together for five more minutes before Ben dared move again. By then, Kyle's hands were loose at his sides and the noises changed to the light sounds of a sleeping child.

Ben looked at his son. How could the kid go from hysterical to sleeping? Ben's heart was still pounding and he felt ready to jump out of his skin. Yikes. What had he done to the kid? He'd ruined what had been a good moment with Kyle, one of the few times when he felt they were truly bonding and having fun together. Then he had to go and hoist the kid in the air, scaring him.

How was he to know what Kyle liked and what would scare him? This parenting business was all trial and error. He so did not want to screw things up, but it looked like he was doomed to just that. Poor Kyle to be stuck with such a parent. He hadn't exactly lucked out with his mother either.

Ben covered Kyle with a heavy comforter, a thing his grandmother had made when he himself was just young. Kyle slept on. Ben went to the kitchen to make some grilled cheese sandwiches for them.

When they were ready, he brought a tray with lunch into the living room. Although he'd assumed Kyle was still sleeping, he was sitting on the floor, his head precariously close to the sharp corner of the thick glass coffee table. His eyes were fixed on the TV screen where Dora the Explorer gets a puppy. Kyle seemed unaware that Ben had entered the room or set down the lunch tray. Ben called Kyle's name three times, each with no response, each with rising frustration. The television wasn't on that loud. What was the matter with the kid? Where did he get off thinking he could ignore his father like that?

Again, reason asserted itself and he remembered what Ms. Nicols had said. Show, don't tell. Well, he had no pictures on him, but he did have the sandwich. He moved it in front of Kyle's face. Kyle reached for it. Ben held it back, waiting. Kyle reached again. Ben prompted, "What do you say?"

"Please," Kyle responded.

Ben gave it to him. Well, at least they were getting somewhere. He corrected himself. It was obvious that Kyle had learned basic manners long before he came to Ben's house. Ben just needed to learn how to prompt his son to use them. He was getting better at it; they both were.

They ate their lunch in silence, watching the adventures of Dora. Kyle continued to watch; Ben dozed. He was startled awake by movement beside him. Kyle had left his spot on the floor and crawled onto the couch beside Ben. He snuggled in and didn't stir when Ben moved his arm to put it around his son. His weight felt warm. His hair smelled like little boy. Ben drifted back to sleep thinking that Kyle had forgiven him for that ill-advised air toss. Maybe he could make it as a father after all.

Mel sat in her car. "Breathe," she told herself. "In through the nose; out through the mouth. Practice those calming breaths." How could she teach her students calming strategies? How could she handle any crisis her class threw at her, yet could not get through one dinner with her family in peace?

Once upon a time, they had weekly family dinners. Mel would spend Sunday afternoon and evening with her parents and brother. But these last few years, the tension had grown so thick; she could only bear to come once a month at the most. Come to think of it, they no longer invited her any more than that. Well, at least they were all on the same page on this one point.

She slipped out of the car, more pressing her door shut than slamming it, hoping no one heard the sound. She felt guilty trying to sneak in, but it was the only way. She walked on the grass, muffling her footsteps, around to the side door. No one used this door, but her brother.

Grinning, she picked up the miniature oil can she had left under the steps several months ago. She squirted a few drops on each of the hinges, replaced the can, then carefully opened the door. No squeaks.

Inside, she avoided the middle of the old steps and made her way down the stairs. Once at the bottom, there was no need for stealth. The basement suite had been well sound-proofed so her parents upstairs would not be disturbed by Jeff's activities. Her older brother still lived at home and spent almost twenty-four hours each and every day within these basement walls.

Picking her way across the room, Mel avoided the piles of dirty (or maybe they were clean - who could tell?) clothes on the floor. Jeff wouldn't care if she stepped on them, but his acute hearing would immediately tell him if her foot trod on a CD case or any of the electrical components strewn around in what Jeff insisted was an organized fashion.

Stopping within a foot of him, Jeff was oblivious to her presence. His gaze was intent on the computer screen in front of him. He focused on just the one, ignoring the programs flashing on the other two. Mel's heart sank as she recognized his avatar.

Jeff was playing Second Life™. The online game advertised itself as the place to connect, to work, to explore, to be different and to be yourself - all the things Jeff wasn't good at in the real world. For Jeff, this game was his world. It made Mel's blood boil. What a waste. What a crime. And, she placed the blame squarely on her parents.

Knowing better than to startle him, Mel moved into Jeff's peripheral vision. No response. She moved closer, calling his name and pressing into his side.

"Yeah, yeah, I'll be with you in a minute. I can't stop right now," Jeff told her.

Melanie sighed. She wondered how long he'd maintained that stiff posture, head and shoulders tilted toward the screen. She looked at his hair. It was clean, and he didn't smell so likely he'd not spent all night doing this, although it had happened before. Often.

"Okay. I'm good now. I just had to finish that part," Jeff explained. "How are ya, Mel?" He gave her shoulders a quick hug, carefully keeping only his arm in contact with her body.

In return, Mel put both arms around her big brother and gave him one quick, hard squeeze. He tolerated it.

"I'm good," she said. "What's new with you?"

That started Jeff into a detailed monologue about some new activity he was into on Second Life. Once he got going on a topic, it was hard to derail him. From experience, Jeff recognized her signal. Mel held up one hand between them, in a stop motion. Since they were kids that had been their signal that he was talking too much and needed to let her have a turn.

"Oh, sorry, Mel. It's just so neat that...."

"Stop!" Mel told him. That's not what I meant when I asked you what was new. I meant in the actual world, not on the computer.

"Are you going to start that again? Geez Mel, you just got here."

"I'm sorry Jeff. It's just that I worry about you. You're my big brother; you're way smarter than me and you're stuck here in this basement."

Jeff's shoulders turned away from her. His eyes returned to the computer monitor where a screen saver flashed his avatar. She was losing him.

She tried again. "Didn't you tell me you were going shopping last week?"

"Yeah. The latest version of...." and he was off and telling her about the newest game he had bought. Mel sighed. Jeff played computer games. Jeff created computer games. He taught himself programming languages to enhance the games he had. And he did all this with no formal training.

Jeff had two passions - computers and cooking. As he was growing up their parents let him do the former but not the latter. The kitchen was their mother's domain and rare was the occasion when she'd allow Jeff to "mess it up". So, any cooking Jeff did, he did at Mel's house.

"Are you spending the weekend at my place? If you give me your list, I'll get the groceries."

Jeff rummaged through the papers scattered on his desk and produced a coffee-stained print-out. "Remember to get exactly what I wrote down," he reminded her. "Is there anything there you don't understand?"

From experience, Melanie knew it would take her days to scour the city for all the ingredients on Jeff's list. He took his inspiration from the food network on television, and some of the items were not exactly the staples found in normal households. But, when she tasted his creations, the shopping efforts were worth it.

She had something specific on her mind. "Would you make me something special this time? There's a new kid in my class. He and his dad came over to play with Max. He's kind of a lost kid and doesn't have a mother. I tried to make him some chocolate chip cookies, but they were nothing like yours. I'd like to have some on hand in case he comes again."

"Since when do your students come to your house?"

"Oh, never mind. Is supper ready? I suppose I should go say hi to the folks."

"Yeah, I'll be with you in a little bit. I just have to do some more here..." and Jeff was back into the world of Second Life. Watching him, Mel didn't know if she was more mad or sad at what his life had become.

Her mother looked over her shoulder when she heard the basement door open. She stirred the sauce on the stove. "Hi, honey. Nice to see you," she began. Then she looked closer at her daughter's face. "Oh. You're not going to start that again, are you?"

"God, mom, how can you stand to see Jeff just sit there day after day when there's a big, wide world out there and he has all this talent?"

"He's doing what he wants."

"How does he even know what he wants? He's never had the chance."

"No, he didn't have the same chances you had. It's different. You weren't born with autism; he was."

CHAPTER 9

A little after ten the next morning, Ben dropped in at the condo to welcome Millie. She was pouring herself a cup of coffee.

"Any regrets, Millie? Is this arrangement going to work for you?" he asked.

"I'm looking forward to spending time with the little one, but right now, I'm relishing the peace and quiet of your place. Then I'll start picking up around here and...."

"Yeah, sorry about the mess. We had a bit of excitement last night. Actually, more than a bit.

"I did something really stupid," he confessed. I was going to fry us some steaks so I heated the oil in the pan. Then the phone rang and I got caught up in talking with my sister, Ellie. You've met her before."

Millie nodded.

"While I was on the phone, I guess Kyle came into the kitchen and saw that the pan was smoking. I can only guess what happened next, but I heard him screaming and came in to find the pan on fire, and a tea towel on fire, wrapped around Kyle's arm. I panicked."

"Oh the poor little lamb. Is he all right? Is he here?" Millie got up to go to Kyle.

"I don't know how, but he's all right, just one burn on a finger. His shirt was trashed but I think I got to him in time and all that happened was his skin was a bit reddened on his arm. When I think of what could have happened, what almost happened...Kyle deserves a better father than me. I almost caused a fire and he could have been killed."

"Do you think you're the first parent who has ever forgotten a pan on a burner?"

"It's inexcusable. A parent is supposed to take better care of his kid."

"Yes, you're right. But all of us do the best we can at the time. Kyle's okay, you said."

"Yeah."

"Did he seem traumatized by the whole thing?"

"No. That's a funny thing. I certainly was, but he seemed okay. Ellie came over and she was less shaken by it than I, but then, she wasn't here and it's not her kid."

"When I arrived this morning, it smelled faintly of smoke. I looked around but couldn't find anything wrong."

"Well, if you look, you'll find one less frying pan in the cupboards."

"We'll survive that, I imagine. But these walls look a bit dinghy. It takes a special compound to wash away the traces of smoke. I'll bring some with me tomorrow."

"You don't need to do that. Tell me what to get and I'll pick it up. It's my mess you're cleaning up."

"And it's my job to be the cleaning lady."

"Thanks. Millie, I don't mean to be rude, but you look a bit tired today. Are you all right? Is this job going to be too much for you?"

"I may be almost old enough to be your mother, but I'm not that old. In fact this job and working at just one place and looking after a little boy all seem like less work than I've been doing these past few years. I love Kyle already and you've always been good to work for."

"But...?"

"It's nothing to do with you and this job. My nephew, my late husband's brother's eldest son is living with me. His boss relocated him here just for six months to oversee the opening of their new branch. He's a dear fellow. So are his wife and four children. They couldn't find a house big enough for them all that didn't require a one year lease. He didn't want to spend that kind of money when they're only here for six months.

"My house is huge, as you saw and there's just me in it, so I told him they could move in with me. I can use their rent money to get started on some of the repairs that need doing. I know you noticed them; I could see it on your face."

"Sounds like a good arrangement."

"It is. And, I shouldn't complain. It's just that I'm used to being alone even though I do get lonely and complain about how quiet it is in that rambling house. Now, it's not quiet. Oh, no. Two more adults and four kids certainly fill up a place. There is always noise, music playing, the television on, someone running up and down the stairs, kids bickering, the fridge opening.

"Listen to me. I sound like a cranky old woman. I can see that they are trying, really trying not to be intrusive, but I'm the one who feels like she's intruding on their space."

"Sounds rough," Ben said. "At least it'll be quiet here as soon as I shove off and before Kyle gets home from school. Even then, he's a pretty quiet kid. When he's not screaming, that is." Then he added, "But I think the screaming happen less often now and maybe doesn't last as long. Either I'm getting used to it or getting better at heading things off."

Ben put his cup in the dishwasher, picked up the mail and headed back upstairs to work.

Unusual for him, he had trouble getting his mind back into his files. Sorting through the mail, he spied the monthly condo board newsletter. Ah, that should either put him to sleep or make him eager to get back to work.

The newsletter included a list of the number of people waiting to purchase condos in this building. Good to know in case he ever wanted to sell. The newsletter also included a listing of any condos for sale at this site. Ben saw that the penthouse was available. Hmm. Those things didn't come up often. The owner had to leave the country temporarily and was looking for a tenant for eight months, beginning next week. Ben winced when he looked at the rent they were asking. Other than the price, maybe that's where Millie's nephew should have moved his family, leaving Millie to the peace of her own house. But then, the penthouse only had three bedrooms. Three bedrooms plus three bathrooms and a small den.

Ben paused. Could this be the answer to his problem about Kyle not having a room of his own? Three bathrooms for just the two of them might be a bit much, but it was more space and still in the same building so he was close to work. Maybe it would take him five seconds more in the elevator, that's all. Ben continued to read the description. This suite came with a wrap-around balcony, each eight feet by ten feet long on two sides of the condo. A concrete balcony wasn't quite the same as a backyard for a kid to play in but at least it would offer some fresh air without having to go outside the building.

Ben did some calculating, something accountants were good at, naturally. He'd bought his condo when prices were in a slump and things had risen considerably. Judging by others for sale in the building, he could get almost double what he'd paid for it. And, thanks to his fanatic work hours and hoarding of money, pre-knowing about Kyle, the condo was well on its way to being paid off. Putting in double the required payment every month paid off. Actually, considering what he paid into his mortgage, he could just about swing the penthouse rent. And that would give him a few months to figure out where he wanted to live.

Three bedrooms, three bathrooms. I wonder, Ben mused. The timing was right. He called the building manager.

Ten minutes later, he and the manager shared an elevator ride to the penthouse. The owners had already left for Europe, putting their belongings in storage. Ben prowled the empty place, thinking about possibilities. Yes, if he and Kyle took the two smaller bedrooms and offered the master suite to Millie, she'd have her own bedroom/sitting room and bath. He wondered if she might even remotely consider moving in with them, being a live-in housekeeper. That would solve her problem of living with her nephew's family and certainly solve Ben's child care problem. She'd be getting free room and board plus her present salary, in exchange of looking after the house and Kyle.

He'd need to be careful about giving her her own space and any time off she wanted, but it just might work. It would certainly free up more of Ben's time to work. The den was small, but if he organized it properly, it would be a fine place to work at home, without needing to run back to the office in the evenings. The den opened off the living room, without even a door to mar his view of Kyle playing.

"Millie, will you come with me a minute? I'd like your opinion on something." On the ride up in the elevator, he told her of his frustrations over his condo being too small. While it had been fine for one man alone, having Kyle changed things. Millie had noticed, boy had she noticed, she said.

Ben showed her the master suite last. As she exclaimed over its spaciousness and view on two sides and how the furniture could be arranged, Ben worked up his courage to present his idea.

"Listen, no obligation at all. I want your honest opinion. If you don't like the idea, we'll stick to our original arrangement. I just thought that it might be a solution to both our problems, at least temporarily."

"Okay, Mr. Wickens - Ben, get on with it."

When he outlined his proposal, she was quiet, too quiet. Ben started to back pedal, fearing he might lose Millie all together.

"No, you have it wrong. I can hardly imagine living in such a grand place and yes, this seems like an answer to my prayers. Are you sure about it? This seems a hasty decision."

"The paperwork might take a bit of time but I could put in an offer today. We'd need furniture and I'd need to list my place, but I don't think there will be a problem selling it. It was a show home and I could sell it with all the original furnishings."

"It's a deal, then. My nephew and his family, dear as they are, will be pleased to have my house to themselves."

Now that Millie was fetching Kyle from school in the afternoons, Ben found that he missed that job. It was the few extra minutes he had with his son, Ben told himself, nothing to do with passing the time of day with Melanie. If he did enjoy seeing Melanie, it was for the tips about managing his son that he looked forward to.

It was Friday and over a week since he'd seen his son's teacher. It was time to probe her for more hints. Millie was heading back to her house to have dinner with her nephew's family and to pick up a few more of her things. The family's van had fold-down seats that would transport some of the furniture Millie wanted to use in her new room in the penthouse. Ben was heading to the school for Kyle.

He came half an hour early - not a tardy father, he thought. That gave him time to slip into the back of the room to watch. Watch his son, of course, not his son's teacher. His timing was good, giving him a chance to watch a lesson in How Does Your Engine Run?®, part of the Alert Program®,. It was always the way Melanie started off the school year. That way the kids all used the same terminology and were on their way to learning ways to manage themselves.

Ben leaned against the back counter, after waving to Kyle, and listened. The children were giving Melanie examples of when it was all right for their engines to run high, like at recess, when they should be low, like before falling asleep at night and when their engines should be in the middle, like right now. On the white interactive board at the front of the room was displayed a gauge that resembled a car speedometer. Kids pointed to various places on the gauge to show where they felt their engines were right now.

Then the discussion changed to things the kids could do to alter their engine speeds. They gave a number of examples, many of the children pointing to things they used in the classroom, like the different seating options and the weighted products. One kid talked about Theraband™, something new to Ben. He watched as the little boy said, "See?" and demonstrated with his feet. Attached to the front legs of his table was a stretchy band. The student put his feet on it and pushed back and forth. Well, if he seemed to think it worked for him, at least it was a quiet activity that wouldn't bother anyone, Ben thought.

Jordan, the child who had given Ben the Hokki™ to sit on that first day of school kept watching Ben. His steady gaze made Ben squirm. He hated to think that he wasn't comfortable with people in wheelchairs and likely that wasn't it. The kid just kept staring.

Jordan called out, "Ms. Nicols, Kyle's dad is wiggling too much. His engine is running high and he needs to do something about it." All eyes turned to regard him, making Ben fidget even more. Melanie grinned at him, enjoying his discomfiture.

Lori weighed in. "What would you suggest he try?"

Answers popped up from all around the room. "Eat something crunchy. Sip water through a straw. Chew gum. Sit on a ball. Sit on a wiggly cushion. Use a lap weight."

Melanie looked at Ben. "So, you've heard the suggestions. Which do you think might work for you?"

"Would running out the door work?" he asked.

The kids giggled. Kyle got up and dragged over Melanie's Hokki™ stool. Jordan said, "It worked for him before."

Ben planted himself on the wobbly stool and tried to find his balance. He so did not want to fall on his butt in front of Melanie and Lori and all these little kids who were expertly perched on all kinds of contraptions. He got the hang of it, continuing to wiggle, just a little.

"Feel better?" Melanie asked.

Ben gave her a sardonic look of thanks. In a few minutes, actually, he did feel better.

As the kids filed past their teacher, each pausing for their, "hug, high five or handshake", Ben waited just outside the door. He wanted to talk to Melanie before taking Kyle home. He looked up to find Lori watching him, amusement on her face. He looked away quickly. What did she know? A father would do a lot for his son, wouldn't he and it certainly didn't hurt that the source of his advice was not bad on the eyes.

But as the last child left the room, Melanie hustled off down the corridor. He called after her and she gave the one minute signal with her hand, but kept going. Ben and Kyle stepped back into the room, Kyle heading for the beanbag chair and bookshelf area.

"She'll be back soon," Lori told him, "She has a lot to battle right now."

"What do you mean?"

"You haven't heard the controversy? About how some parents are trying to shut this classroom down?"

"Why would anyone do that? Even I can tell that the kids are happy here and progressing. Just look at Kyle. She's a fantastic teacher. Why would anyone want her fired and what can I do about it?"

"It's not Melanie they're trying to get rid of, but this classroom. It's the whole integration concept they don't like."

Ben looked blank.

"Look," Lori continued. "Haven't you noticed how small this room is, how there aren't very many kids in it? Most kindergarten classes would have half a dozen more kids. And most schools would have a class for typical students then another room for only those with special needs."

"Like Jordan?" Ben asked about the most easily identifiable child.

"Kids like Jordan and like Kyle," Lori corrected. "In this room we have eight kids with special needs and eight typical kids. Plus me, the educational assistant."

"Eight kids with special needs. Which ones are they?"

"Hah! The point exactly. You can't tell. That's the point of integration and from students learning together. Life is not a segregated affair, they're all going to have to learn to live together and learn from each other.

"But some parents don't see it that way. They fear that the special needs kids will take up so much of the teacher's time that their precious baby won't receive enough attention and progress at the proper rate. I could tell them that their kids are going to end up further ahead than those who are in a straight K room."

"K?" Ben asked.

Lori smiled. "Kindergarten. Sorry – school lingo." She continued. "The other issue is money, of course. The parents' group complain that this program is too expensive, having two adults in the room for just sixteen students. But they're getting a bargain. My salary is half of what they pay a teacher. If this room wasn't here, they'd still be paying Mel to teach the special ed class. I'd be out of a job, or at least this job, but they'd probably end up putting me in the room the eight typical kids get moved to because thirty K kids all together is too much for one teacher to manage.

So, there would be no money savings, just one crowded classroom and one half empty one."

"So what's Melanie doing about it?"

"She's meeting with the principal right now. Dr. Hitkin supports this room and she's a staunch supporter of Mel, but this goes farther than her power. Parents have gone to the school board and there's a meeting tomorrow night."

"What happens if things don't go the way you want?"

"Then come Monday or at least the following Monday, this classroom will look very different. It might have just the eight special needs kids in it and the other students will be dispersed into the other classroom. That would make that room overcrowded and the parents' precious children would get even less attention than they fear they're receiving now."

"What can I do?"

"Well, if you really want to help, show up here tomorrow night at half past seven, in the gym. Just the moral support of parents coming out will help Mel, even if things don't go the way she's fighting for."

A young man came to the door of the classroom. Ben moved aside and the man drew Lori, the EA, toward the back of the room. Something about the guy made Ben take another look, but Lori smiled as the guy kissed her cheek lightly, so Ben withdrew, giving them some privacy.

Several minutes later, he poked his head in again, hearing raised voices. After all, his son was still in the room. He didn't like the look on Lori's face; her usual, open grin was missing along with her confidence. The guy had a grip on her arm. As Ben watched, Lori pulled back but didn't get far as the guy tightened his hold on her. He heard Lori tell the guy to leave her alone; she didn't want to go with him tonight.

That was enough for Ben. He was about the guy's height, but had twenty pounds and ten years on him. It might not be his business but he could not stand to see Lori intimidated by this dude.

"I heard the lady tell you to leave her alone. Step back, please," Ben said.

The guy looked him up and down but didn't loosen his grip on Lori's arm. "Who are you?" he asked.

"A friend." He put threat into the words. "Now, step back and let her go."

"Ben, please, it's all right," said Lori, although her eyes didn't tell him to go away. Ben stood his ground. "I told you to let her go," he reminded the man.

The guy eyed the two of them, weighing his options. He released her arm, giving it a shake. He retreated with, "I'll see you later."

Ben asked Lori, "Is that all right? Do you want to see him later?"

"It's all right. We used to see each other but I've been kind of backing off lately and he isn't taking it that well."

"He looks like someone you might want to be careful of. Are you sure you're okay?"

"Yeah, thanks. You know, we weren't sure at first, but Mel's right. You are a nice guy." Before Ben could ask what she meant by that, she was gone. Had Mel actually said he was a nice guy?

Melanie returned to the classroom, walking too fast. Lost was the relaxed air she had around the children. She stopped short, surprised to see Ben still there. Was he that forgettable, he wondered? Apparently so. The look on her face worried him. "Are you all right?" he asked.

"I am, or I will be. It's just that some people are so short-sighted. What we're doing here is good and it's right. All the kids are benefitting."

"You don't have to sell me."

Melanie looked at him skeptically. "I thought you didn't want your son in a classroom with those kids?"

Ben sheepishly remembered the things he had said that first day. Well, when you're wrong, you're wrong. So, he said, "I was wrong. I didn't know. Kyle is exactly where he should be and he's already doing so much better. I'm doing so much better. Thanks to your help and your ideas, my son and I are all right. I gotta tell you, those first few days I didn't know if we were going to make it."

Melanie relaxed and smiled at him. "You would have been all right. I didn't know about you at first, and wondered if you were the sticking around kind. It's not easy to raise a child with an autism spectrum disorder and some parents bolt or fold under the pressures."

Ben looked offended that she would think he'd be like that. Then he remembered that that's exactly what Kyle's mother had done. Well, Kyle was his for good now and nothing could pry them apart. Ever.

Watching the expressions flit across Ben's face, Melanie had the impression that this guy really was a keeper. For Kyle, of course, she meant.

"That brings me to why we're still here. You've already helped me so much with Kyle and I appreciate the time you've taken. But I'm going to ask another favor of you, if you have the time. I know this is a lot to ask but I don't know who else to turn to." He hesitated.

"Go on."

"Look, the place we're living in is awful. It's not actually an awful place and it wasn't for a bachelor who's hardly ever at home. But for a child it's just not right. We're living in a two bedroom condo, but the second bedroom is my office. Kyle's sleeping on a fold-out couch in that office. The room's small and already full with book shelves, a desk and the couch. There's no room for Kyle's things, he's living out of a suitcase and there's no room for him to play."

He had her full attention, so went on. "The living room looked okay to me, prior to being a father. The furniture is all white leather. There's a white carpet and in the center of the carpet is this glass monstrosity of a coffee table, perched on some kind of sculpted base. The glass is about a half inch thick with pointed corners. I've cracked my shins on them a number of times but I'm worried Kyle will knock his head on one. When he plays on the floor, his head is close to those corners."

Okay, he was babbling. Get to the point. "So, I'm going to sell the condo. We're moving into the top floor condo in my building. It has three bathrooms, three bedrooms and a small den off the living room. Millie, the woman who used to cook and clean for me twice a week has agreed to move in with us to help with Kyle. She'll have the master suite and space of her own. She's a widow with her own house, but her nephew and his family moved in with her for six months and she's finding it crowded."

This was way, way too much information. Something about this woman made him nervous. "So. I'm going to sell my condo as is, with all the furnishings. It was a show suite that some big deal decorator did up. But the new place is empty. I need furniture and I need it fast."

He looked appealingly at her, hoping she'd sifted through all this and figure out what he was asking. Obviously not, because she just looked at him. Try once more. Why was this so hard? She'd either say yes or no and what did it matter? It's not like he was asking her on a date.

One last try. "Will you help us?"

"Help you what?"

God, she must think he was an idiot. "Help us furnish the place. I have no idea what a kid needs and you seem to know so much about kids in general and Kyle especially. I want a home that's comfortable for a child, not some designer show piece that even I'm not comfortable with." He tried to grin. "Please?"

She grinned back. "When?"

When? It was that easy? Why did it take him a huge monologue when all it would have taken was one sentence? "Tomorrow." He hastily added, "If that's all right with you. I thought we could go shopping and have lunch or something. To pay you back for helping us, of course."

"Sure." They grinned at each other until Kyle's weight leaned against Ben's leg. He was tired of waiting.

CHAPTER 10

Kyle and Ben were in the park near where they'd agreed to meet Melanie the next morning, indulging in some more leaf-jumping, leaf-throwing while they waited. Across the way they spotted Melanie, sitting on a bench overlooking the pond, her back turned to them.

He had an idea. Signalling to Kyle to keep quiet, he grabbed an armful of leaves, gesturing for Kyle to do the same. Then he pantomimed tiptoeing and the two Wickens men advanced stealthily towards the unsuspecting woman. When they were close enough they each let out whoops and threw their leaves over Melanie's head. Too late, Ben at the last minute remembered that women didn't like getting their hair messed up and Melanie might be mad at them. What if she hated having bits of dirt and crawly things on her head? What if she refused to go shopping with them? What if she refused to hang out with them ever again?

Melanie turned around, looking at one then the other of them. Then she grabbed her own handful of leaves and tore off after Kyle, mashing leaves all over his head. They fell to the ground laughing together. Then Mel whispered to Kyle and they both turned to look at Ben. He backed up with both arms outstretched as they advanced on him. Not paying attention to where he was going, the back of his knees hit the bench and he sat down, hard.

Instantly, Melanie was on him from behind, holding his shoulders down as Kyle threw leaves all over him, all over all of them.

Well, at least she didn't seem mad.

Brushing themselves off, they headed back toward Ben's condo, so Melanie could take a look at the space they were going to furnish. Kyle walked between them, reaching for each of their hands. Ben glanced over to see if Melanie minded, but she was relaxed, probably far more relaxed about holding the hand of a child than he was. Every so many steps, both he and Melanie would raise their hands, giving Kyle a swing in the air. Unlike the time Ben had raised him toward the ceiling, Kyle liked this ride.

No, Melanie wasn't mad. She even seemed to be having fun with them. Like a family. Now, where did that thought come from?

As they entered the lobby, Kyle led the way to the stairs. Ben tensed. He'd totally forgotten.

The first time he tried to get Kyle into the elevator, it had been fine until the car started to move. Kyle totally freaked. Totally. Ben had been unprepared and even if it happened again now, he'd have no idea how to cope. He had solved the problem by forsaking the elevator for the stairs from then on. Or, at least whenever Kyle was with him. Climbing three flights of stairs would keep him in better shape anyway. Right? And although it might seem like a lot of steps to an adult, a five year old seemed to handle them no problem.

But what now? The penthouse was on the fifteenth floor. There was no way they were going to trudge up all those stairs. Ben looked helplessly at Melanie, fresh out of ideas. He seated Kyle in a lobby chair and pulled Melanie to the side to explain the problem and how he'd gotten around it so far by taking the stairs. Melanie threw him a disapproving look, as if this was his fault. Well, what was he supposed to do? And how were they going to get Kyle to the penthouse now? He had not thought about that at all when he signed the papers to lease the new condo or when he'd signed to put his present condo on the market. What had he done to them now?

"Do you have any paper? A pen?" Melanie asked?

"What?" Ben didn't understand.

"Pen? Paper? You know that stuff we use to write?"

Ben sighed. He reached in his pocket and gave her his pen and a small notebook.

"Huh. Moleskin. Nice," she said.

Quickly Melanie sketched out stick figure drawings of the three of them standing close together in a little box. She drew an arrow pointing up. "I'm making Kyle a social story," she told Ben. This did not seem like a social moment to him, but whatever. She did seem to know how to handle Kyle.

She explained to Kyle what an elevator did and gave him far more details about the pulleys and operating systems than Ben thought any small child should have to hear. He was surprised that Kyle listened intently. She then showed him her drawing and hurriedly made another one.

"Kyle, today you have a choice. Today, you have a choice. You can ride in the elevator two ways. Remember in class when we read that book about the monkeys and how the baby monkey clung to its mother?"

Kyle looked at her unblinkingly. Melanie seemed to think he was following her.

"You have a choice. You can ride in the elevator standing between your daddy and I, holding our hands. Or you can ride hanging on to the front of your dad, just the way the little monkey did to its parent. And, any time during the ride you can change your mind and ride standing or with the tight hug.

"Then when we get out of the elevator we're going to see the new condo. We'll measure it to see how big the stuff we buy should be. I will need your help holding the tape measure."

She stood, took his hand and led him to the elevator door. He tensed and started to pull away. She shoved the picture she'd drawn in front of his face and repeated her story, pointing out Kyle, Ben and herself in her drawing. Having averted crisis number one, she engaged Kyle's attention with the elevator buttons. She had him push the up button.

"Now watch it. Watch closely and you'll see it change color. When the color changes we'll hear this little ding sound. Right after that the doors will open and we'll get in. Once inside, we turn around and will see more buttons. I'll tell you which one to push. Now watch that button closely, please and tell us when it changes color."

Through her machinations, they actually got inside the elevator. She instructed Kyle about which button to push; Ben had to lift him up to reach the P for penthouse. They were fine even when the doors closed, but not when the elevator started moving. Kyle tensed and put back his head to howl.

Melanie got on her knees, so her face was level with Kyle's and placed her hands firmly on Kyle's shoulders, pressing down. His eyes were wide with fright. "Kyle, Kyle," she said. "What is your choice - standing with us or monkey ride?"

Kyle couldn't seem to form any words. Melanie repeated the choices. Kyle turned to his dad and raised his arms. Ben reached down, and enfolding the little boy in his arms, stood. Melanie arranged Kyle's legs around Ben's waist and his little arms around Ben's neck. Kyle's face was buried between Ben's chin and collar bone. Breathing was a problem for Ben, part from the squeeze of Kyle's arms, part from being overcome with emotion himself. His son was terrified, yet trusting Ben to protect him. What a responsibility. What an honor. Over Kyle's head, Ben's eyes met Melinda's. "Thank you," he mouthed.

Melanie inspected what seemed like every visible inch of the condo, approving of Millie having the master suite and taking measurements of the living room, den and Kyle's room. Ben's room he could do himself, she told him. It needed his personal touch. What would she say if he told her he'd like her personal touch in that room? Banish that thought, he told himself.

What Kyle ended up with was not what Ben had imagined. The pieces Melanie chose were of good quality, sturdy but not overly pricey. She bypassed the bright-colored shiny pieces, saying that Ben wanted Kyle's bedroom to be a quiet retreat, a place conducive to relaxing and sleep. But there were fun pieces and plenty of places to hide. His bed looked like a circus tent, albeit a taupe big top. No gaudy colors. The bed section was reached by scaling steps at the end - nothing like the ladders from bunk beds of Ben's childhood, but these ones were an actual set of stairs running along the end of the structure. There were handrails and the steps were enclosed on the sides so Kyle wouldn't fall off. As a bonus, each step was a storage box with a pull-out drawer. Nice touch. The top bunk was draped with a circus high top curtain. Melanie insisted that Ben climb atop with Kyle. When he protested that it might not bear his weight, Mel said then they'd better find out now before they bought it. Gingerly Ben climbed the stairs and stretch out on the bed, testing its solidity before allowing Kyle to join him. Once inside, it felt cozy like they were in a tent. There was a clear window so Kyle could look out and the drapes could be pulled back if he didn't want them.

Under the bed was a walk-in area that contained a child-sized desk, chair, lamp, book shelves and storage areas. Again, this area had curtains that could be opened or closed, depending on the child's mood. And, best of all, the side of one curtain had a flap that could be opened if they wanted to put on an old-fashioned puppet show.

The closet would have built-ins with an adjustable hanging rod at Kyle's height now that could be raised as he grew. Instead of a chest of drawers, clear pull-out bins would hold the rest of his clothes, clear so Kyle could see what was in each container.

For reading and lounging, Melanie selected an adult sized bean bag couch, big enough for two cuddly adults, an adult and a little boy or several children. Melanie chose storage bins, all again in that same taupe color that would hold Kyle's blocks and puzzles and toys. There were similar ones in bright oranges and reds and greens but Melanie vetoed them in favor of dull colors that didn't stand out. "Trust me," she said, "You'll thank me later." Ben certainly did have a lot to thank her for.

The living room ended up with leather again, but not white. These were butter soft brown couches that invited you to sink in and cuddle up. A flick of the levers at either end of the couch turned that seat into a recliner with foot rest. Ah, what a way to watch the game.

There would be a coffee table, yes, but no more glass with sharp edges and nothing precariously balanced on a base. Solid wood with rounded corners and inset tile on the top. Easier to maintain than wood when small children spill their milk and juice, Melanie explained.

Ben's stereo equipment would have a safe home with components that Kyle would use easily within his reach. There was no point in putting them higher because Kyle would just climb to reach them. He was going to use them anyway and had already shown his proficiency.

The rest of the condo furniture came together quickly. The den was furnished as a work space for Ben, yet with space for Kyle. Mel explained that since Ben would likely be spending a lot of time in there, Kyle would want to be with him and Kyle would want to mimic his dad. So there was a big desk and a child-sized desk. There were storage shelves for Ben's books and shelves for Kyle's books. Ben had a matching filing cabinet and Kyle had a not-quite-so-matching storage cabinet with pull-out bins instead of drawers.

This place was going to have such a different feel than his present condo. It would feel like a home, something that was currently missing. Ben hadn't really noticed before since he spent little time at home anyway and even less time thinking about his surroundings. In fact, he gave so little thought to decorating that when it had come time to furnish his offices, he hired the same decorator that had done his apartment. He did this not because he was particularly enamored with her style, but because she was the only decorator he'd heard of and her business card happened to be posted in the lobby.

Much as Ben thought he hated shopping, this had been fun. They'd actually played in the stores, bounced their butts on countless sofas and pretended they were sitting on the couch eating pizza and watching TV. Cheese pizza only Ben had remembered, earning him a grin from Kyle and a head on his arm. Ben hid his face hoping no one would see just how much this gesture from Kyle meant to him. Melanie saw, though, but didn't comment. She kept her thoughts to herself, grateful that no one knew how watching Ben with his son affected her.

Lunch had been gyros at a mall food court. Glorious, messy gyros they enjoyed, Kyle especially getting as much on him as in him. The adults did not escape the sauce and Melanie reached with a napkin to wipe some off Ben's cheek, before drawing back embarrassed. He said, "No, go ahead. I can't see it there." She continued, not meeting his eyes, his not leaving hers. She made a show of cleaning up their tray and saying they needed to get going if Kyle didn't want to end up sleeping on the floor.

At one point Ben had become so used to Kyle holding each of their hands that he automatically reached for a hand when they left the store. To his surprise the hand enfolded in his own was Melanie's. Kyle appeared on his other side and took his hand, grinning at both of them. Ben grew red and started to apologize. Melanie squeezed his hand but didn't withdraw. She didn't meet his eyes but left her hand there. Ben didn't know how the day could get better. His son's teacher was really something. A good sport, smart and practical. And beautiful. The kind of woman a guy could get used to.

He stole a glance at her. What was she thinking? Was she just doing her duty for one of her students, one of her more needy students, considering what a dud his father was? Of course that's what it was. This woman was a true teacher, dedicated to her profession and to the kids in her charge. Look how she'd lit into him each time he screwed up with Kyle. Yes, she was doing this for Kyle since the poor kid had such a clueless dad.

Melanie herself wondered what in the world she was doing. She had a firm policy to keep her professional life and personal life separate. She never dated anyone she worked with. And, she most definitely never dated the parent of one of her students. That would be unprofessional. She could not recall any school board policy against it or anything in the teaching code of ethics, but certainly it just made sense.

Plus, this meant nothing to Ben, she was sure. He had asked for her help because he didn't know where else to go. Obviously he could not rely on the decorator who had furnished his sterile, impractical condo. She shuddered, remembering how it had looked. Definitely not the environment for a young child or anyone for that matter who wanted to be comfortable.

Yes, Ben had been right to ask for her help. She knew Kyle and she knew kids and she knew autism. That combo was what he needed. That's all this was. She should not delude herself into thinking there was any more to it than that. Sure they'd had fun. Why not? Why make shopping drudgery. Yes, they'd had fun in the park. Why not? Didn't even harried businessmen need a chance to unwind and play sometimes? That's all there was to it. He'd been playing with his son and she just happened to be nearby. The whole day felt so good just because she'd been under stress with this whole school board thing. That's all there was to it.

The plan was for Ben and Kyle to drop Melanie off at her home so she could get ready for the school board meeting that evening. But the adults had not counted on one little boy and one big dog. Max was waiting for them when the car drove up and he was wild with excitement to get at Kyle. Kyle was just as anxious to get out and romp with Max. So, Melanie and Ben ended up sipping glasses of wine on the back deck while boy and dog raced up and down the enclosed yard, indulging in a game with rules that were a mystery to all but the two of them.

The sun was losing ground on the horizon. The leaves were tinged with autumn colors. The two lounging in the chairs were mostly quiet. But, it was a good quiet, the kind where companions didn't need to fill the space in order to be comfortable and content in each other's presence. Ben didn't know when he last felt this relaxed. Well, yes he did - the last time he and Kyle were here at Melanie's. In fact, he'd felt so relaxed that time that he'd acted like a jack ass and fallen asleep on her. Smooth move, dude.

He asked her, "Have you forgiven me for passing out in this chair last week?"

She laughed at him. "You looked cute while you slept."

Hmm. Was that how he wanted her to remember him? Cute? What about handsome or manly or even hot? Cute was a long way from any of those adjectives. He'd need to work on his approach some more.

What was he thinking? Work on it? Why? Did he actually care what she thought of him? Well, of course he did. She was his son's teacher and they'd become friends of sorts. Did it matter that all she thought of him was that he looked cute sleeping and he was Kyle's dad? Yes, it did, it certainly did seem to matter.

"What?" Melanie asked. "Why are you looking at me like that, like you're sizing me up?"

"I'm thinking about what you said and I'm not sure I'm happy with you thinking I'm cute."

Melanie was embarrassed. "It's just a figure of speech. I didn't mean anything by it. I'm not coming on to you or anything."

"Why not?"

"Why not what?"

"Why aren't you coming on to me?"

"Jeez, Wickens, what are you talking about? We had a nice afternoon. Let's just relax and not spoil it."

Ben continued to watch her. "Would doing anything more spoil it? Or could it make it even better?"

"This is not the time or place. Kyle's watching." As she said those words, Kyle and Max raced around the side of the house. They could hear his squeals and laughter from the front yard now. "Thanks, kid," Melanie muttered.

Ben grinned. "I don't see you running away after him." He leaned towards her. She didn't move. Ben took Melanie's wine glass and placed it on the floor between them, along with his own. "I think we'll hear those two coming before we see them." He leaned closer, giving her time to pull away if she chose to do so. She didn't. In fact, she seemed frozen in place, staring at him. His hand reached behind her head, caressing the back of her neck, while looking into her eyes. Still, she didn't move. Ben put pressure on her neck, drawing her head closer. He lowered his own head then closed his eyes as his lips met hers.

Oh, thought Melanie. Oh. This was better than she had imagined and yes, she had imagined what this would be like if it ever happened. His lips were warm, his cheeks slightly chilled from the air, the taste of the Riesling on his tongue.

Wait! This wasn't right. She was a teacher with ethics and principles to uphold and this was the father of a student. She couldn't do this.

"Melanie?"

"Y-y-es," she stammered.

"Don't."

"Don't what?"

"Think. Don't think. Just quit it." And he went back to kissing her. Melanie, never one to take orders willingly, obeyed. And enjoyed.

CHAPTER 11

Ben was early. Ellie was staying with Kyle and he had wanted to make sure he got a seat with a good view of Melanie.

He was certainly not into these kinds of meetings, or meetings in general that weren't absolutely needed for his business. He had almost not come, thinking it wasn't a big deal. When he'd said as much, Melanie had looked at him like he'd lost his mind.

She'd said that if it did not go the way she wanted, come Monday, Kyle's school world would look different. The classmates he'd come to know would be gone, or at least half of them. Lori would be gone. Mel would be there, hopefully, although even that was not a foregone conclusion. She might be sent elsewhere and a new teacher would take her place. Other special needs kids from around the district might be imported into the room. Maybe their exact room would shift and the remaining kids would be put elsewhere in the school or even in the district. Life as Kyle knew it would most definitely change.

The gym was not full but there were certainly more people there than Ben anticipated. He'd thought since there were sixteen kids in the room, maybe thirty parents would come, tops, then a couple school board people, the principal and Melanie. Instead there had to be at least four times that many people. The buzz of conversation was electric. Maybe this wouldn't be quite the boring Parent Teacher Association meeting he'd thought it would be.

In a row of chairs along the front were a handful of men and women in suits, board members he assumed, plus Dr. Hitkins the principal and Mel. Actually, the description that came to mind first was his Mel. A day ago he would have knocked that thought out of his head fast, before it had time to take root. But today, considering the afternoon they'd spent together, maybe, just maybe, it was not so wrong to let his thoughts drift in that direction.

Ben had always assumed he'd have a wife and family one day. Even the white picket fence bit didn't scare him off. But all that seemed so far away, a one day dream. It might have moved closer toward that dream if the right person had come along, but that had never happened. Hell, what chance was there of meeting someone when all he did was work twenty-four seven? Nah, his work wasn't to blame. That was his choice and he liked it, the challenge, the drive, the hours and the feeling of success.

Then Kyle had burst into his life. Well, he had part of the dream now, just not in the order he'd thought and not in the manner he'd wanted. A planful person, Ben liked to be in control. He thought things out, made a plan, took charge and followed the path he'd laid out. It worked, always had for him. Then, Kyle. Nothing about Kyle was planned. Well, perhaps his conception was planned by Deanna, but not by Ben.

Ben was not in control with Kyle. In fact, the little man had blown into his life and taken over control. Did that mean he was a chip off the ol' block? Ben smiled to himself. The kid certainly did have a will of his own. No, Ben was not in control but that feeling was not as scary as it was a month ago. Although he knew that as the parent, he had to ultimately make the rules, his household was evolving into more of a shared power place where it was not all about Ben anymore, but life flowed around a pint-sized person. And, that was not so bad, he was discovering.

Mel was a lady who also liked to be in control; that was evident in her classroom. His original opinion of her had been wrong. The opinion had been honestly earned, the way she had glared at him at first and told him off each time he screwed up. He had deserved some of that, maybe more than just some. What he had seen as just bitchiness had really been her fierce protectiveness of the children in her charge. She truly cared and not just about their progress as students in her class, but cared about them as people and how they'd get along after they finished their year with her.

She cared. That was one of the first things you noticed about her. She even cared enough about Kyle and how he'd settle into his new life with his stranger father, that she'd offer assistance from how to run their home to how to furnish it. She really did go over and beyond what any teacher should have to do.

That was why she'd agree to go shopping with them, wasn't it? Or could there be anything more? Did she do this for all her students? Doubtful. But then, most kids wouldn't have such clueless parents.

Ben detested shopping - always had, always would. But, today had been fun. Rather than impatience with the waiting and the crowds and the time it took, he'd had fun. Honest fun. Why? It's not like children's furniture stores were exciting places to be, nor was a mall his idea of a hang-out place on a Saturday afternoon. But, the company had been good - great, in fact. Spending time with Kyle and Mel, what more could a guy ask for?

The meeting was called to order, just in time. His thoughts were heading in a strange direction best left uninvestigated.

Listening, Ben learned that Kyle's classroom was not usual - it was an experiment, the brain-child of master teacher, Melanie Nicols. It was her belief that students with special needs learned best in the company of their age peers, not in secluded classrooms without typical role models. On top of this, she also believed that typical students would also benefit from being with their counterparts who had extra challenges.

She said that while in our grandparents' generation, different may have been seen as wrong or needing to be hidden away, society has changed. Not only are we multi-cultural, but multi-ability. People with physical and intellectual handicaps are living and working with us. Kids with special needs who spend their entire school life in segregated classes will be less equipped to manage in the adult world. Typical kids who have grown up rubbing shoulders with those who have more challenges will be comfortable with differences. They will have learned to lend a helping hand when needed. Even more importantly, they will have learned to see past what lies on the surface and see the abilities that may be less obvious.

As the meeting progressed, research citing the benefits of integration for all students was explained and written copies were ready for anyone who wanted in-depth reading.

One father stood and asked just how much this experiment was costing them.

Dr. Hitkins, responsible for budget matters, talked about the economics. It was a given that all children deserved and must be provided with an education. That included all the children of the adults in this meeting, whether the child had a special need or not. It was the law. All these students would receive a free, public education.

In a school that had a segregated classroom, there would be a teacher, an educational assistant and a small number of special needs children. The number was set by state law; the adult/pupil ratio was small. For example, in Madson School, there would be a teacher such as Ms. Nicols, and an educational assistant with eight children.

The other eight students currently in Ms. Nicols room would have been with the other kindergarten class, bringing their total number to thirty-two - a lot of little ones in one room.

Being well aware of these numbers and having spent her Masters of Education work studying service delivery models, Ms. Nicols proposed combining classes. In addition to the eight special needs kids assigned to her room, she offered to take an additional eight students. There would still only be a total of sixteen children, far less than the anticipated thirty-two. This would also bring the numbers in the other classroom down to just twenty-four. The cost was still the same to outfit the two rooms and pay the salaries.

The benefit was to the students in the smaller classroom - all the students. Teachers like Ms. Nicols go through the traditional training common to any educator. But on top of this, Ms. Nicols had a specialization in exceptionalities. Her studies included disabilities of all sorts, on top of master teaching techniques, the kinds that benefit all children. Her training looked at methods of assessing an individual child's strengths and challenges. And, make no mistake; all children had strengths and challenges, just as did every adult in this room. Ms. Nicols was especially suited to looking at each child as an individual, designing and providing individualized programs to move each child along as far as possible. In her arsenal were far more than the usual range of teaching methods. These were extra sets of skills possessed only those taking advanced training in exceptionalities. All the children in her room this year benefited from her individualized approach.

Dr. Hitkins pointed out that no two of us learn alike. We all have strengths and weaknesses, ways that appeal to us and approaches that cause us struggles. Ms. Nicols took each of these facets into account and designed lessons tailored to the way your child learns best, and at the same time exposing them to other ways. While we have many talented teachers in our building, none has as much training as the teacher nurturing your children right now.

Some parents initially opposed to this classroom and wanting it shut down, became quieter. Still others adamantly demanded changes for their kids. They worried that their children were not receiving the attention they deserved. They worried that the curriculum would be watered down to a level far below their child's skill level. They worried that the kids with special needs would demand all the teacher's time and attention. What would happen to their kids in the next grade if they had not covered the kindergarten program?

To address this concern, test scores were projected on the screen. While names were removed, the audience could see where students were in September in the basic areas covered by the tests. Then overlaid on top of this were the mid-year scores. Everyone could see that every child had progressed. For some, the progress was slight; others had moved leaps and bounds. The lines were rarely even. Each child seemed to be moving at their own pace, some gaining half a year or more in the two months, others gaining the expected two months while a few moved only a couple weeks' worth.

Despite this evidence of progress, some nay-sayers still muttered.

Ben was not a public speaker, far from it. Although he'd make his opinions known in a meeting when warranted, his preference was to gather behind closed doors with his subordinates, debate and hone their collective thoughts, then let his staff present the consensus at client meetings. He'd found it worked well, built their confidence and skills and it certainly did his firm no harm to have him remain in the background unless needed.

But, this was different. He'd had no closed door meeting to prep ahead of time. And the way this gathering was going, things would go downhill for Kyle, for Melanie and for the other kids. Not only for the sake of his son, but for the other kids in the class, Ben felt he must offer his two cents to the discussion. He rose.

"At the beginning of the year, I shared many of your opinions. I took one look at the classroom they were putting my son in and said that I didn't want him in with those kids." People turned to look at Ben, a couple applauded. Dr. Hitkins frowned at him; Melanie glared.

He continued, "I was put off by the mixture of students in the room. I didn't even notice the low number; I was so out of touch with school systems that I didn't even know it was unusual to have just sixteen kids in a kindergarten room. I thought the economy had hit this school hard because kids didn't even get their own desks - they had to share tables. And, I thought the school couldn't afford proper chairs because the kids were perched on all sorts of things like one-legged stools, wobbly plastic stools, balls, cushions - all strange things to my eyes.

"The first time I observed, this kid - a little kid in a wheelchair kept staring at me. It made me uncomfortable, and I guess I was restless. The kid finally told the teacher that the man in the back was squirmy and needed a Hokki™, whatever that was. The teacher said, 'Good idea'. I ignored him. Then there's the sound of an electric motor and the kid somehow propels himself to this larger plastic stool that's tilted to one side. This little kid leans way out of his wheelchair to grasp the stool in his arms because he didn't seem able to lift with his hands. No one helped him. I thought that here's this poor little handicapped boy struggling and no one helps him. The kid got the stool onto his lap and wheeled it over to me. He made it obvious he wanted me to sit on it. I did. You know, the kid was right. I did need that crooked, wobbly stool. When I sat on it, I was less restless and my attention focused on what was going on at the front of the room. The kid watched me a few minutes then returned to the lesson. The others just carried on as if all this was normal. I didn't even thank the kid, something I still regret.

"That's the way this classroom operates. They observe each other and help each other. All of their contributions are considered and appreciated. They all have something to offer.

"I watched another lesson, one the kids call "How Does Your Engine Run™" from the Alert Program®. The language and concepts the students used were far more sophisticated than I'd dreamed of from five year olds. They were talking about keeping their engines or their attention at just the right level, revving high when they were out for recess, low when it was time for bed and in the middle when working in school. They offered each other suggestions for how to raise or lower their engine speeds. I saw five year olds, barely more than babies, getting things, doing things to help themselves work better. More importantly, they were not just following the teacher's directions, but figuring out for themselves what they needed to do and then just doing it. Oh that some of my employees would exercise that judgment." That brought a laugh.

"I'm new to this world of special needs and I came with lots of preconceived notions. I thought normal kids did stuff and other kids should do other things. I had limits in my mind of what certain children could or should do.

"My son has autism. I consider myself a bright enough guy, and like many of you, I have a college education. I'm a businessman and own an accounting firm. My son is five. We play chess. Try as I might, I rarely win. That kid whomps my ass." Some in the audience laughed, others turned to look at him. Ben didn't care.

"My ideas of what certain kids can and can't do were wrong. I set limits. I assumed that since my son does not talk much, he does not think much. I was wrong. I thought that because a kid was in a wheelchair that he couldn't think, or that he'd have nothing to offer me. I was very wrong.

"In my company, there are certain things I look for in employees. I want self-starters. I want people who can think independently. I want people who can work as part of a team, who can problem-solve, who can work their way through conflicts and present ideas. These are the sorts of things I see happening in Ms. Nicols classroom and to a degree that blows my mind."

"I see the beginning of these things in your children when I visit their kindergarten classroom. The door is open and any of you would be just as free to observe.

"We live in a multi-cultural world now days. This includes multi-abilities, as Dr. Hitkins said. Even more than we do, your children will need to understand and get along with all sorts of people.

"What do we want from a school? I think that we want our kids to become educated and to have the skills to find a job afterwards. These are the things our kids are learning in Ms. Nicols' inclusion classroom. I would not want my child anywhere else." Ben sat down.

There was silence. And silence. Then in the far corner the sound of a clap was heard. Then another, a second later, followed by another after the same wait. That lone clapper was joined by another, then another until much of the crowd clapped along, the pattern long since lost. Some parents stood, and soon a standing ovation filled the room. While not all parents stood or clapped, the critical mass tipped and the class was safe.

Ben slipped out the back door as the meeting broke up and the panel at the front surrounded Mel.

Mel puttered in her kitchen feeling lighter than she had in months. She had not realized just how heavily it was all weighing on her. The thought of losing her class was too hard to bear. She'd feared that they wouldn't understand the progress the kids had made - all the kids. They'd become a community together, learning together, helping each other, playing together. Each and every one had progressed. Some were farther ahead than their counterparts in the regular kindergarten class down the hall. An integrated classroom, with the proper supports, did not hold anyone back. It was a win-win situation.

But she and Dr. Hitkins had worried about how to get that across to the public and to the school board. The kids had been tested up the wazoo and yes, they had the proof on paper that the students were learning at at least the expected rate. But how to demonstrate that without putting the audience to sleep with statistics, comparisons, graphs and test scores?

Inviting parents and board members to visit the classroom hadn't worked. Few actually came. Few that is, except Ben.

Ben. Help had come from an unexpected quarter. Ben had saved the day with his speech tonight. Who woulda thunk it? she said to herself.

Boy, had she misjudged him. Her first impression had been of a dead beat dad. The mom had gotten tired of single parenting and tried to make Ben own up to some of his responsibilities, dumping Kyle on him for a change. She'd assumed he was the kind of guy to take no interest in his child, to leave the hands-on child care to others.

Well, she was right in her assumption that he knew nothing about his son. That much certainly was obvious. He had not known his son, but as she later learned, that was through no fault of his own. Still, could he not have made more of an effort to be involved in his son's life? Perhaps he was telling the truth when he said he'd stayed away at Deanna's request so as not to confuse Kyle with two daddies. Maybe. And, he had said he supported them financially once he learned of Kyle's existence.

She smiled to herself. Ben. He'd looked uncomfortable at the parent-teacher meeting, certainly not a place he'd envisioned for himself. But when he spoke, people listened.

A part of her wanted to think that he'd stood up to defend her. That would have been nice. But realistically, why would he bother? She was his son's teacher and yes, she'd given him advice about Kyle, but it wasn't anything more than that. Couldn't be.

So, why was she conflicted? One part of her was proud professionally that Ben had defended her class and her teaching because she was good at what she did. He liked the changes he'd seen in Kyle and attributed them to Mel's teaching. He spoke so definitely and so eloquently that he'd swayed the crowd and her room was safe. Yes, he'd done it for his son's sake. Surely that was it. It only made sense.

A small part, a teeny, tiny part, buried way down deep in her heart wanted Ben to have done that for her. Not for any philosophical belief, not for the sake of his son, but for her. Because he cared and wanted to support her.

Okay, get rid of that thought.

She took her tea and snuggled back against the pillows. What kind of reading was she in the mood for? She had a new Janet Evanovich book on her bedside and a new John Locke book on her Kindle ereader. Hmmm.

Locke it was. There was always some vague romantic thread running through Evanovich's books; less so with Locke. Any hint of romance might make her examine her own life too closely and that would make her think of the afternoon she'd spent with Kyle and Ben.

That must be what it felt like to be a family. Kyle was such a sweetie. She grew close to all her students, felt like they were part her own. But it was different with Kyle; he was special. Maybe it was because he came to her such a lost soul, dumped by one parent and faced with this second parent who was a stranger. A stranger with no idea what to do with a child. They'd needed her. Her advice, that is.

Ben had actually listened, listened far more than she'd ever expected. He'd not only listened, but he took her advice, trying out each approach, reporting back on how it worked, and asking for help in refining it. On top of that, he'd researched and read on his own. When he came with fresh questions, they were intelligent and thoughtful. He really wanted to learn and he really wanted to help his little boy. It showed.

He was also not the stuffed shirt in a suit she'd first assumed. Watching him cavort in the park with Kyle had opened her eyes. There was more to him than a stiff businessman. He took his responsibilities to his company seriously, and he took on the responsibility of fatherhood just as seriously. But he was more than just serious. He knew how to have fun and play with his little boy.

He knew how to have fun with her, as well. Yes, the three of them had definitely had fun shopping today. Ordinarily she was an in and out kind of gal when it came to shopping but they'd dawdled and browsed and enjoyed the day. Who would have thought an uptight guy like Ben could unbend and have fun?

Drats! Her mind had wandered back to Ben again. Enough. Relax with some chamomile tea, find out how Donovan Creed was doing in the Locke book, and then have a good sleep. Her class was safe and that worry, the constant need to prove herself, was over.

Although Creed's adventures and misadventures usually held her rapt, not so much this night. Her mind wandered to lunching with Ben and Kyle, bouncing on mattresses as they tested out beds for Kyle, the pillow fight he'd had with his son. Yes, her thoughts were about Kyle and Ben as she nodded off.

CHAPTER 12

E llie gabs too much; she always was a pest. That's the thought that went round and round in Ben's mind. It had been a busy week then a big day shopping plus the meeting at the school tonight. The tension in the gymnasium had been palpable and now Ben was tired. He just wanted to go to bed.

Kindly, Ellie had stayed with Kyle while Ben attended the meeting. She'd bathed and put her nephew to sleep. There was silence in the condo, or at least there would be if Ellie quit talking.

She was pestering him with questions, questions to which he had no answers. And, he didn't even want to think about such questions. She wanted to know about Mel, Kyle's teacher.

It seemed that Kyle had been unusually eloquent that evening, telling Ellie about their shopping spree, having lunch with Ms. Nicols, throwing leaves with Ms. Nicols, playing with Max, going to Ms. Nicols' house and on and on and on. All this information had Ellie honing in on Mel and Ben, wanting to know what was going on, what there was between them, and where this was headed - all questions Ben could not answer.

Luckily, siblings can be blunt with one another and Ben finally told El that he was going to bed. She was welcome to stay over or leave but he was tired and had had it for the day. Being the little sister, one who had learned the art of self-preservation while growing up with older brothers, Ellie knew when to pull back and regroup, waiting for another day to come at Ben again with her probing. She decided to go home but in her parting shot, said she was leaving so things would not be awkward if Mel came over the next morning. Ben sighed.

Sleep didn't come as easily as he'd hoped. Ben tossed and turned. Damn his sister. Her probing had struck a nerve and made it impossible for his thoughts to turn away from Mel. Every time he closed his eyes, there she was. His mind had a snapshot of her standing in the tree-dappled sunlight with her hair full of the leaves Ben and Kyle had thrown on her, her head thrown back laughing. Then there was Mel bouncing on a mattress in the store with Kyle. She lifted Kyle high in her arms so he could bonk his dad on the head during their pillow fight. Mel holding Kyle's other hand as they swung him along the sidewalk. Mel offering them warm cookies. Mel watching his son play with her dog. Mel leaning back in her lawn chair, her eyes watching his as their lips met. Yes, these were not the sort of thoughts destined to lull a man into sleep.

Ben woke with a start, his legs tangled in the sheets, his bed a wreck. What woke him up? There it was again. What had he heard? There. That noise. And movement. Someone was in the apartment. Kyle! He had to protect his son.

Hurrying out of bed took more work than usual, with his covers wrapped around his limbs. But he got out and searched the floor for his sweat pants. He felt vulnerable enough with a small child in the apartment; he didn't fancy facing an attacker stark naked.

Thankful for the thick hallway carpet, he crept towards the faint sounds. The kitchen was dark but there was enough illumination from the streetlight to show him that the kitchen was empty. The study with Kyle on its fold-out bed had its door still closed, just as it had been when Ben checked on Kyle before he went to bed himself.

Next, the living room. There was a faint glow and yes, the sounds were louder now. At least he was now in between the sleeping child and whatever he might find in the living room. Ben flattened himself against the hallway wall and peered into the room. No, nothing at eye level. But, looking lower, the glow came from the television. It was on. Someone was watching his TV.

Peering closer, Ben watched an animated little girl with a big head and monkey pal dancing across the screen to the music. Faintly, he could hear, "D-D-D-D-D-D-D-Dora...". Kyle! That was one of Kyle's shows.

Approaching the back of the couch, Ben could see not see the top of anyone's head - the couch was empty. Looking down, the flicking images on the television showed a small shape on the carpet beside the coffee table, that glass monstrosity the decorator had so raved about. There was Kyle, out of bed at two-thirty in the morning watching his Dora the Explorer™ DVD.

Disconcerted to see him, but relieved that they had no intruder, Ben bellowed, "Kyle!"

Kyle, engrossed in his show, had not heard his father's approach and was startled by the yell. His head swiveled around quickly, so quickly that his left temple whacked the sharp corner of the glass coffee table. There was silence for the space of three seconds, then either the pain of the bump or the surprise of Ben's yell caused Kyle to let out his own bellow. Just as that sound began to die down, Kyle noticed the blood.

Oh, the blood was everywhere. Ben had heard that head wounds bled profusely but surely no one meant like this. Maybe the white of the carpet made the growing stains more glaring. Maybe the widening pool spreading on the surface of the glass table made it worse. You could see the blood both on the table and in the pool beneath it. Worse though was the crimson soaking the little boy's purple dinosaur pyjamas and the worst was the rivers of blood coursing down the side of Kyle's tiny face. He screamed as one trickle of blood flowed into his eye, stinging him. Ben didn't know if the child was crying from pain or fear.

But, to Ben, it looked like his son was dying. He felt like wailing right along with Kyle. No. He had to keep it together. He had to get help for Kyle. He had to save his son.

He scooped the small boy up in his arms and cradled his head. Kyle clung to him, sobbing and bleeding until they were both covered in blood. As Kyle wiggled, Ben had more and more difficulty holding him snuggly as they became slick from the blood.

Right. First he had to get help. Nine-one-one. No, he could not stand waiting here until the ambulance came. They weren't far from the hospital, he'd take Kyle there himself.

First aid. What were you supposed to do with bleeding wounds? Cripes, he couldn't think. Ben had always considered himself calm and efficient, a cool head in a crisis, but all that had deserted him now, now when it mattered the most.

To the bathroom. He ran with Kyle in his arms and sat him on the bathroom vanity. A quick rummage brought out bandages. Bandages. How do you put one on when the skin is flowing with blood? Quick, think. What to do, what to do? Okay, pressure. Yes, that's what you're supposed to do. Apply pressure to help stop the bleeding. But how do you press on a little boy's head, especially when there is a gaping wound on that same head?

A towel. Ben's brain slowly started to function and he grabbed the damp towel off the nearby rack. He balled it up and pressed it gently to the cut, holding Kyle's head steady with his other hand. Kyle leaned against him, crying softly. Ben's heart rate slowed just a notch, enough for him to let out the breath he'd been holding and raised his eyes to the mirror.

What he saw ratcheted everything back into overdrive. Both he and Kyle looked like something out of a war-ravaged conflict. Ben's chest, shoulders and face were smeared with blood, some spots drying, others glistening in the bright vanity light. And Kyle,

Kyle looked worse. His new pyjamas, selected by Kyle and Mel that very afternoon were unrecognizable. They were sodden and stiffening and dark red. His hair was matted with blood. There was so much blood on the right side of his face that a first horrifying glance would make you think he'd lost an eye.

Okay. Deep breath. Don't show your panic or you'll frighten Kyle even more. Think. What to do next. Try to stop the bleeding with pressure. He was doing that. Elevate the wound. Well, he had the kid sitting right side up, so that was as elevated as he was going to get. What else? Oh, right. Keep the wound clean.

What was he doing? How many times had he showered and used this towel, the very one he now held to the open wound on his son's head? He could at least have grabbed a clean towel.

"Hold on, Kyle. Sit right here little man and press this to your head. I have to grab another towel." With a steadying squeeze to Kyle's shoulder, Ben ran to the linen closet to grab a handful of clean towels. Returning, he threw the used one into the tub, folded a new one and gently pressed it to Kyle's temple.

As Kyle calmed and Ben calmed, Ben had Kyle hold the towel himself while he wet a face cloth with warm water and tried to wash the worst of the blood off the rest of Kyle's face, his neck and body. Gingerly he unbuttoned Kyle's pyjama top and rinsed off the drying blood.

"Are you all right to sit there a minute bud while I get you some fresh clothes?" Kyle nodded and Ben raced to the den. Once again he cursed the fact that his son was living out of a suitcase. It was too hard to find things in. Frustrated, Ben upended the suitcase, spilling the contents in a half circle around his feet, rummaging until he found a fresh top for Kyle. He grabbed his jacket as well.

Kyle had not moved and his crying had all but stopped. He watched Ben with big, trusting eyes that made Ben's heart break. How had he let this happen to his son?

He lifted him off the vanity onto the floor. Then he changed his mind and picked him up in his arms. He was not going to let this child out of his grasp.

Carrying Kyle into his bedroom, he set him on Ben's bed while he grabbed the first shirt he could find to put on his bare, bloodstained chest. Okay, they were ready for the hospital.

Picking Kyle up again, he walked with him to the closet where their coats were kept. As he removed the towel to help Kyle into his jacket, the bleeding began again in earnest, starting to soak the clean shirt. This was not working. How was he going to drive and hold this towel to Kyle's head, especially when Kyle was supposed to sit in the back seat in his booster seat where it was safest? Ben couldn't do it all. He needed help.

Mel. The name came immediately to his mind. He needed Mel. Oh, it was so true, he really did need her, in every way.

Would she come? If he called her, would she come to help him and to help Kyle? It was iffy if she would actually come out in the middle of the night for him, Ben, but she just might do it for Kyle. She was a devoted teacher and really did seem to care for the kid.

He tore his cell phone off the charger and dialed with one hand. His other held the uninjured side of Kyle's head firmly to his side with the towel pressed against the gash. He moved the towel slightly to take a look. Yes, the bleeding might be easing off again.

Come on, come on, Mel. Answer the damn phone.

"Hello?" came the sleepy question. "Who is this?"

"It's Ben. We need your help. Kyle's cut his head and it's real bad and we have to get to the hospital. Would you meet us there?"

"I'm on my way," was the reply, and then there was just dial tone in his ear. Despite the situation, Ben smiled to himself. His panic felt cut in half with just hearing those four little words.

Now, how to keep the towel firmly in place while he drove. Ben's eyes roved the kitchen searching for answers. His gaze lit on the junk drawer. Ah, ha. He eased Kyle that way and opened the drawer. Yep, he had some. He carefully folded a fresh towel and held it in place. He got out the scissors and handed them to Kyle, showing him how to hold them. Wait. This wouldn't work. They'd never get the stuff out of Kyle's hair.

He remembered seeing a cap when he dumped out Kyle's suitcase. He picked Kyle up and ran back to the den. Yes, there it was. Nope, that wouldn't work. With the cap on, there was no room for the towel. He threw the now bloody cap on the floor.

Back by the door was a cap of Ben's. Yep, it was big enough. Carefully holding the folded towel in place, he gently placed his hat over top of Kyle's head, towel and all. It fit. Sort of. Kyle turned to look at him, knocking the hat sideways, then half off. Not going to work.

Deep breath, try again. Back to the original idea. Towel in place. Dad's hat on. Kyle wielding the scissors, Ben the roll of tape. Round and round and round he rolled the tape around Kyle's head, holding both the towel and hat in place. Just for good measure, he wound more tape across the top of Kyle's head, down across his shoulders, under his armpits and back up the front side to meet on the top of the hat. Goofy looking? Perhaps. But would it hold things in place during the ten minute drive to the hospital? Probably.

"We're ready, bud. Let's go." Kyle resisted the pull of Ben's hand. Now what? This was not the time for the kid to get stubborn. Kyle tried to remain rooted to the ground. When Ben bent down to pick him up, Kyle told him, "No."

Ben bit back a curse. The kid had been through a lot. This was not the time to lose his patience with him. Kyle struggled to get out of Ben's grip. Ben let him for a second and ran his hands over his face in frustration. Kyle bent into the closet and returned with his shoes. He then threw Ben's out as well. Ben just looked at him. They were both in bare feet and it was late autumn outside. Which of them had kept their head? Kyle grinned at him. And, off they went.

Ben pulled up to the emergency room door, parking alongside an ambulance. He unstrapped Kyle from his seat, lifted him into his arms and ran through the sliding glass doors. He paused only momentarily, deciding which way to go. A passing nurse, spotting the copious amount of blood once again covering both Ben and Kyle pointed him in the right direction, saying, "Go, go!"

Ben ran, Kyle's uninjured temple pressed hard into his dad's shoulder, Ben's one hand cradling the bleeding side, pressing on the hat and towel. Kyle, whose crying had pretty much stopped, whimpered in the bright lights and the unfamiliar smells. A passing intern's rubber soled shoes squeaked on the freshly washed floor, making Kyle struggle to free his hands to cover his ears. He buried his face in his father's shirt.

Just as Ben again hesitated, unsure where to go next, there was Mel. She stood waiting for them. One step behind her was a nurse, obviously alerted to their arrival. Mel half turned to her and beckoned towards Ben, confirming the nurse's guess that this was the case Mel had told her would be arriving soon.

Thanks to Mel's intervention, there was no sitting in the waiting room. They went right in, laying Kyle on a gurney draped with a thin, light blue sheet. Overhead was a light enclosed in a two foot diameter dull metal casing with handle grips on either side.

The nurse leaned over Kyle and smiled. "What have we here?" she said.

"He cut his head on the side of the coffee table. It's heavy and sharp and has no business being in a room where a little boy plays. This is entirely fault."

The nurse just looked at him.

"Too much information," Melanie muttered. Ben started to speak but she shook her head at him.

The nurse ignored them both. "Let's take a look. Hmmm. How do we get this hat off of you?"

Mel looked from Kyle's head to Ben. "Duct tape?" she asked. "All you could think of was duct tape?"

"Well, it worked, didn't it? And, I was pressed for time." Ben said, his posture defensive.

Kyle stayed still, with only the odd tear on his cheek until the nurse murmured that she'd need to cut the hat to get it off. Kyle let out a yell.

"It's okay, bud. She's only cutting the hat, not you or your hair. It's okay, sh, sh, sh," Ben soothed. His words had no effect.

Mel thought a minute then stepped up. She asked the nurse for just a minute and pressed her hands firmly on each of Kyle's shoulders. "Are you worried about your dad's hat?" she asked.

Kyle quieted and looked at her. Someone had understood.

She continued. "It's your dad's old hat. He was going to throw it out anyway. He has other ones, better ones. And, I think he was planning on buying a new one, a special hat that comes in your size and his size so you can both wear the same hats when you go out.

Kyle's gaze zoomed in on his father's face. Ben nodded and confirmed that what Mel had said was true, even if this was the first he had heard of it. It did not sound like such a bad idea, anyway. "And maybe we could find one for Ms. Nicols, too."

Kyle smiled at his teacher and held his head still. The nurse started cutting and cutting and cutting, glancing up at Ben several times as she did so. "You didn't want this to fall off, did you?" she commented.

Ben would have defended himself again but he caught Mel ready to laugh at him. He smiled sheepishly in return then moved his gaze back to Kyle. His hand hovered close to his son's head as if he was ready to snatch the scissors from the nurse's hand if she so much as harmed a hair on the child's head. Mel, noticing Ben's jumpiness, reached over and took his hand. The gesture startled Ben, causing him to look at her in surprise. She kept her gaze on Kyle, but squeezed Ben's hand reassuringly. He squeezed back then folded his fingers around hers. It felt good, almost like they were in this together.

As the nurse cut through the layers enough to unearth the towel, she gently tried to pull it from Kyle's temple. He moved his head away, resisting her attempt and clamped both his own hands to the make-shift bandage.

Mel looked at Ben. "Did you tell him to keep that towel on his head?"

"Yes. I needed his help to keep pressure on it. I had to drive, you know."

"Kyle, you did a good job of helping your dad. But he only meant that you had to hold it until you got to the hospital. You're here now so it's okay to let go. The nurse needs to take a look. She'll help you."

With the towel relinquished, all three adults leaned in for a closer look. Ben felt sick. It was so much worse than he thought.

To Melanie, it was not as bad as she had feared. Ben's voice on the phone had sounded on the verge of panic, like this was a life and death situation. That's the way she had prepped the triage nurse, expecting the worst.

The nurse tut-tutted a bit then bustled about finding swabs and disinfectant. "We'll just wash this up a bit so we can have a better look. The bleeding's almost stopped now."

Almost stopped, Ben thought. He could clearly see it still seeping out the cut and running back through Kyle's tousled hair. Some lodged in the whorls of Kyle's ear; some ran on behind and onto the thin pillow.

The nurse moistened a swab then began dabbing at the cut. Her dabs were swift and sure and firm. Too firm, in Ben's opinion. He moved to grab her hand. Again, Melanie interfered, scowling at him. "Look at Kyle," she hissed in his ear. "Does it look like it's hurting him? Don't make him any more scared than he is."

Ben looked. No, Kyle was relatively relaxed; certainly more relaxed than Ben himself felt. He shifted his gaze to what the nurse was doing. Now that the area was cleared of dried and drying blood, the edges of the gash were clearly seen. Then the nurse wiped directly on the cut. The edges opened up and she wiped right inside! Ben stiffened and Mel stiffened the arm of her hand that grasped Ben's hand. She held more firmly and turned her body so that it was partially in between Ben and the gurney.

She was blocking him! How dare she? Ben thought. How dare she think that she or anyone else could get between he and his son. Did she think she could stop him from protecting his child? Ben could feel his ire rising. The adrenal that had shot through his body when the accident first happened had not subsided yet and those old adrenal glands were ready to pump out more at a moment's notice. Ben felt his breath quicken. Mel inched slightly more in front of him.

Not that she blocked much. He could see right over her shoulder, over her head for that matter. He looked at Kyle and the nurse's current handiwork. She was still dabbing right on the cut in short, firm bursts. The blood welled, the edges of the wound gaped, the blood spilled, the insides of the skin were visible, the blood flowed....

The next thing Ben knew he was sitting in a chair on the other side of the room. Mel had one arm across his shoulders, the other on the back of his head pushing hard. He was staring at the floor and his head hurt right behind his ear. An orderly or someone or other in hospital scrubs hovered nearby staring at him.

The guy asked, "All right now, fella?"

Who was he talking to, Ben wondered? Why was he asking about Kyle but looking at Ben? Kyle! Where was he? Ben started to get up. Both Mel and the guy pushed him back into the chair. Maybe that was just as well because the room sort of swam when he tried to get up. The guy roughly shoved Ben's head down between his knees again. Ben's heart rate gradually slowed and he lifted his head just a bit.

Mel was kneeling on the floor beside his chair. "Are you all right?" she asked.

Why was everybody asking if he was okay? It was Kyle who got injured, not him. "Why am I over here?" Ben asked.

"Because you fainted."

"What? You've got to be kidding. I don't faint," protested Ben.

From the bed a little voice said, "Daddy fell down. He looked funny."

The nurse agreed with Kyle. Mel tried not to smile. "Can I leave you now and go to Kyle?" she asked.

Just what kind of an idiot did she think he was? Did he need a nursemaid?

"Stay," Mel said, looking at him sternly as she left his side and returned to Kyle's bed.

Now Ben was mad. How dare she talk to him that way? He made to get up. The guy in scrubs warned him, "You better take it easy, buddy. You don't want to take another tumble. They're too busy taking care of your kid to have to look after you again."

Did they all think he was some kind of pantywaist? Sheesh.

Ben glared at the guy and got to his feet. Slowly. They may have a point, he thought. He really did not feel all that steady. He felt the side of his head, surprised to find it tender and a lump starting. He shuffled to the gurney, using the wall at the head of the bed to partially prop himself up.

"Hey, bud," he greeted his son.

"Daddy fell down. You went..." and Kyle gestured with his hands.

The nurse reminded Kyle to lay still.

Just then the doctor walked in, bustling to the sink to wash his hands then slip on sterile gloves. "Now, what do we have here, little man?" he asked Kyle.

"I hit my head. I bled all over me and daddy."

"It looks like you did but it's stopping now. The area looks clean now. What's that hanging off your shirt?"

"Duct tape," Kyle, Melanie and the nurse said in unison. The doctor looked at Ben, the only person who had not spoken. "It's a long story," he told the doctor.

"Head wounds always bleed a lot but most look far worse than they actually are. This one will only need a few stitches and a tetanus shot. In a couple weeks you'll be good as new, with a shiny new scar to show off to your friends."

Kyle was doing remarkably well, obviously better than he himself had done, thought Ben. The doctor explained that he'd numb the area with a salve first so Kyle would not feel the needle going in when he froze the area prior to putting in the stitches. The nurse pulled out the salve, dousing the swab with it. The scent filled the room.

Kyle tensed. His gaze went from adult to adult, trying to figure out where that offensive smell came from. The nurse approached with the swab and Kyle honed in on the culprit. No way was that stuff coming any place near him. He could hardly stand it in the same room let alone on his head. He tensed, ready to let out one of his shrieks.

Mel stepped up fast. She placed both palms firmly on Kyle's shoulders and pressed. That got his attention. She waited until his gaze rested on her face before speaking.

In soothing tones she repeated over and over that he was all right. It just smelled bad but would not hurt him. The bad smell would go away quickly and after his head would feel better. She motioned for Ben to come forward and take her place pressing firmly on Kyle to keep him calm. Kyle gazed frantically from Melanie to Ben, before his eyes settled on his dad.

Mel stepped back and motioned to the doctor. In quiet tones she explained that Kyle had autism and sensory sensitivities. She asked if their x-ray room was nearby. Yes, it was. Was there an x-ray apron they could borrow, one of the heavy, lead-lined ones used to protect patients or technicians? Yes.

In a couple minutes one arrived and Mel draped it over Kyle's body. Quickly, his tenseness drained away and Kyle lay quiet and compliant again. Ben looked at Mel with gratitude.

"Remarkable," the doctor said. He looked at the nurse. "We'll have to remember that trick".

Kyle obviously still didn't like the smell but he made no more protest. The numbing took affect almost right away. The nurse gestured Ben and Mel to the other side of the bed and turned Kyle's head toward them. "Talk to him," she urged.

Mel pulled a children's book out of her purse. Ben looked at her in amazement. Where did that come from? She didn't even have kids of her own, yet she just happened to have a kid's book with her? Anyway, it worked. While they kept Kyle's focus on them, the doctor hid the needle in the palm of his hand, out of Kyle's line of sight. He pressed the tip of the needle against Kyle's skin, watching his face for any reaction. None. Good, the freezing had done its job. He injected the site in several places, handed the spent needle to the nurse to dispose of and readied his materials. By the time he turned back and again made a test prick, the freezing had fully taken affect and he began the stitching.

Ben, watching, felt sick again. But this time he wondered if he was going to throw up, not just pass out. Not that he was admitting he'd actually passed out but he had felt queasy.

Mel again shifted her body, trying to block Ben's view. She put the book in his hands, saying, "Here. Read. It's your turn."

Ben started to refuse, but the steel in her eyes brooked no argument. He read.

"Just one more thing left. Keep reading," she instructed Ben. The nurse pulled down the elastic of Kyle's pyjama bottoms just a bit and swabbed a spot with antiseptic. Then she flicked at the skin.

"One little poke," the doctor explained. Before Kyle realized what was happening and could get out a yell, the tetanus shot was done.

Then, it was over. They said Ben could pick Kyle up and he gladly held the little body tight in his arms. Kyle wanted to see the bandage so Ben carried him to the mirror above the sink.

"Wow!" Kyle said.

"Yep, it's a doosey," the nurse told him. "Better than your dad's."

"Yeah," Kyle agreed. Ben stifled a tiny feeling of hurt. He thought he'd done a pretty good job under the circumstances. He caught Melanie grinning at him.

They moved to the waiting room where they were told to have a seat while the doctor made out a prescription for antibiotics. There were more people waiting there now than when Ben and Kyle had come in. Or, at least Ben thought there were; he really couldn't be sure. It had been all a blur when he was in such a panic.

But now his little boy was all right, or at least he would be soon. Ben sighed. It had been a long, harrowing night. He vowed to take better care of this precious child who trusted his father to look out for him. Kyle shifted on his lap.

Maybe he was over tired, but Kyle certainly was squirmy. He couldn't seem to get comfortable sprawled either on a chair of his own or with a body part on Ben, part of one on Melanie. Initially Ben had apologized to her when his son used his teacher as a chair but she had not seemed to mind.

The small space between Ben and Melanie's bodies seemed to cause Kyle problems. He could not get comfortable. He squirmed to get to his feet and stood surveying the two adults. Then he climbed back into Ben's lap, kneeling. "Careful, guy," Ben reminded him.

Kyle knelt and, making himself taller, grabbed Ben's left arm. He raised it high in the air and brought it down over the back of Melanie's chair. Ben glanced apologetically at Mel. Kyle climbed back down to the floor and surveyed his work. Not quite right yet. Leaning over Mel, he grabbed Ben's hand and put it on Melanie's shoulder. Then he pulled Ben's hand harder, drawing the two adults close together. The space between their bodies disappeared. This must have been Kyle's goal because he climbed back up, laying his head in Melanie's lap and dangling the rest of his body over his father's legs. Within what seemed like seconds, he relaxed and fell asleep.

Ben looked at his son, then at Mel. She looked tired. He brought his hand up to the side of her head and pressed gently to bring her head to his shoulder. At first she put up slight resistance, then gave in and lowered her head. Ben gathered her closer. This felt all right. Definitely all right.

By the time the orderly brought over the filled prescription, Kyle was sound asleep across their laps and Mel's breathing had slowed and evened. Ben guessed that she, too, had dropped off. It felt so good and so right holding the two of them that he hated to disturb them. But, they were sitting under the glaring lights of a noisy emergency room on hard, plastic seats. Only Kyle seemed truly comfortable.

"Hey, guys," Ben gently shook them. "It's time to get going."

Mel came awake, her hair askew from rubbing on Ben's shirt. Kyle turned over but that's about it. Ben hoisted him into his arms and started for the door. Melanie stumbled along beside him. Watching her, Ben thought she was in no shape to drive. Although she'd pulled through when they needed her most, she looked done in now.

"How did you get here?" he asked.

"I drove. My car's in the lot. How'd you get here?"

"We drove. My car's right over..." His voice trailed off.

His car that he hurriedly parked beside the open back doors of an ambulance was no longer there. It was not anywhere in sight. Ben felt his pockets. Neither were his keys anywhere in sight or feel. "Son of a ...." He stared at the spot where he'd last seen his car.

"Maybe it's not stolen. Maybe they towed it away since you parked in an emergency vehicle only spot."

"It was an emergency," Ben retorted.

"I'm not sure the powers that be would see it that way. Let's go back in and see if anyone here knows what may have happened to it. Do you know your license plate number?"

Ben looked at her. "I may have bonked my head a little but not that hard."

When he described his vehicle to the clerk at the night desk, she confirmed that yes, indeed his car had been towed. He could claim it from the city compound after eight-thirty next morning, or rather this morning. And pay the two hundred dollar fine.

Kyle was starting to stir. Ben adjusted him so his head rested more firmly on Ben's shoulder. He asked the clerk if there was a taxi phone around.

"Come on, my car's just in the lot. I'll drive you guys home."

"Are you sure? You've already done enough for us tonight. We really appreciate your help. I really appreciate your help. We needed you."

They were quiet on the drive home. Ben broke the rules since there was no child's seat for Kyle and cradled him in his arms while Mel drove.

When they were almost there, she asked, "What were the doctor's instructions again?"

Ben repeated the doctor's warnings. They were to watch Kyle for any signs that the bleeding was starting again and to check for signs of a concussion. Every two hours Ben was to wake Kyle up. If it was impossible to rouse him at all, they were to return to the emergency room. It was not always easy to tell with young children as they often slept deeply. But if he didn't even stir when Ben tried to wake him, bring him back.

Mel hesitated, let out her breath, and then spoke. "I've been thinking. Kyle's had a rough night but so have you. And you're not going to get much more sleep tonight if you have to keep checking on Kyle. It's my guess that your place might be a mess and there are things to clean up. I don't want to impose, but how about I crash on your couch? We could take turns with Kyle and I could give you a hand with the cleaning."

"You'd do that for us?"

She was slightly embarrassed. "Well, yeah. I really care about Kyle."

"And?"

"And, you could probably use a hand tonight."

Ben let it go at that. There would be time to investigate where this might be going later. "Thanks. We'll take you up on that offer."

They drove in silence a few more minutes. Then Mel looked over at Ben. "Duct tape?"

An hour later the soiled towels were soaking in a washing machine full of cold water and salt. "Salt?" Ben had asked. Melanie assured him that just washing the towels with detergent would set the stain and the blood would never come out.

"So? We'll throw out the towels and get new ones."

Mel's look said what she thought of such wastefulness. And, the towels ended up soaking in half a box of salt.

Ben had rummaged in this drawers and closet for something for Mel to wear to sleep in. All the sweat pants he found were far too huge on her. An old, worn t-shirt was stretched and hung to Mel's knees.

"It's decent enough," she told him.

"Well, it never looked that good on me,' he replied. He didn't have words to tell her how it made him feel to see her padding around his condo, barefoot, wearing just his old shirt. He kept drawing his imagination away from what she might or might not have on under that shirt. She'd done so much for them tonight. He should not have lecherous thoughts about this angel who was his son's teacher. One thing he did know for sure - that t-shirt would never, ever be thrown out. He was not even sure he'd ever wash it again.

They argued over sleeping arrangements. Mel insisted she would be just fine on the couch. Ben insisted she take his bed. In the end, Mel relented, probably seeing that this was one time Ben would not be moved.

It took some time for Mel to lose her grip on consciousness. It has been a taxing day. The first half had been fun, although novel. She'd never before shopped with a man and a little boy and it was not at all what she expected. She'd never spent so much prolonged time in a mall before. And, it had actually been fun. She'd enjoyed the company of both Wickens men.

Her heart had nearly stopped when she awakened from a deep sleep to hear Ben's voice. The near panic had sounded so un-Ben-like that at first she didn't recognize his voice. Then she came fully awake immediately, and threw on the nearest clothes. She raced through the nearly deserted streets, reaching the hospital before Ben and Kyle. She had time to apprise the staff that they were coming with a child bleeding from a head injury.

Then, Ben had fainted. She shouldn't laugh at the guy, but he'd struggled so to be in control then just face-planted.

Boy, had she misjudged him at their first meetings. He really did care about his son, even if he was new to this whole parenting thing. He was willing to turn his life upside down for the child, selling this condo, moving to a place with more room for Kyle, buying new, kid-friendly furniture. He'd talked about his "monstrosity" coffee table and how he constantly banged his shins on the sharp edges. He'd told her how he was always telling Kyle to sit further away from it so he wouldn't bump his head.

And, look what had happened. His worst fears about it. Mel smiled when she recalled Ben's reaction to the white Berber carpet under the table, now stained with blood, likely ruined. He'd hoisted the heavy table onto its side, separated the glass top from the suction cups holding it to the base, stashed the table on its side wedged between the door and another chair, moved the base to the side of the room, then balled the thick carpet up, carried it downstairs and threw it in the dumpster. By the time he got back, Mel had mopped up the blood stains from the hardwood under where the carpet had stood.

Yes, he was a good guy. Far from being a high pressure business man only concerned about his company's bottom line, he had his priorities right. His son came first. Although his apartment was beautifully furnished, the possessions meant little to him. He was prepared to sell them with the condo and buy all new stuff, stuff that would suit a little boy.

Thinking about Ben was not helping her fall asleep. She was in his bed. This was the pillow where he had laid his head only hours before. She turned her face into the pillowcase and sniffed. Ah. It held his scent.

Jeez. What was she doing? Anyone would think she'd lost her mind sniffing a pillow and smiling. Get a grip.

She heard his bare feet on the hardwood as he went yet again to check on his sleeping son. Yes, a good guy all right. She fell asleep holding that thought.

It's not easy to sleep with your head propped high on the rolled arm of the couch and your knees bent over the other arm. When Ben tried sleeping on his side with his legs bent, he perched precariously on the edge of the couch, his legs more off than on. It didn't matter. He did not have much opportunity for sleep anyway, jumping up every half hour to go check on Kyle. Even though he told himself not to and felt himself every kind of a heel for doing so, he also checked on Mel. She'd left his bedroom door half ajar and slept sprawled in his bed. Her hair was loose from its perpetual ponytail and it spread across his pillow. He already knew how soft it was, how the strands felt in his hands when he'd pulled leaves from her hair in the park. Her face was relaxed in sleep, softer, gentler than the Mel he frequently saw. She could be stern, she could really lace into him, and she could laugh and play with the kids. She was many things, his Mel.

His Mel? Where the hell did that come from? He was obviously overtired and needed to get back to his couch.

Ben woke to a whisper then a "Shhhh". Instantly, he thought "Kyle!" He lifted his head, and then regretted it. Oh, his neck. Sleeping at that angle was so obviously not a good thing. The whisper came again, then a giggle. Kyle sounded fine. Then Ben's senses woke up and he smelled the coffee. And, was that bacon?

He unfolded himself from the couch and leaned against the kitchen doorway, watching the domestic scene. Mel was making pancakes, or rather Kyle was. Ben watched him ladle batter onto the hot pan, or rather ladle some batter into the pan and some on the stove top. Melanie didn't seem upset with the mess.

Kyle turned and spotted his dad. He launched himself at Ben, with the total confidence of a child that his father's arms would be there to catch him. And, they were.

Breakfast was a domestic affair, the three of them around the small round table, bumping knees, getting sticky from maple syrup, both adults focusing their attention on Kyle, studiously avoiding each other's gaze. Neither knew what to do with the forced intimacy of the situation.

Well, Ben did. But it seemed too much, too fast. They might really have something here, the three of them and he didn't want to move too quickly or make any wrong moves that might scare Mel off. He had plans for her if only he'd be able to convince her how right they were

CHAPTER 13

The move was on. Once Ben made up his mind about something, he wasted little time. The instant the penthouse became vacant, he planned his move.

It was a matter of faith that his current condo would sell. It had to. He'd committed that money to help pay the rent on the penthouse, plus the sale of the condo would give him a cushion he could use to help Ellie and the bakery. Plus, add to Kyle's college fund and maybe, just maybe build towards a house down payment.

Ben's condo had been the show home of the building. He'd moved in as is, with all the appliances and furnishings the decorator had used to showcase the place. Since he actually did little living there, it was still in pristine condition, largely thanks to Millie's efforts. The only thing that had really changed was the area rug that had stood under the coffee table. That was toast and hauled away to the dumpster. So, he was hopeful that his place would sell quickly and had the realtor's assurances on that. He'd been afraid to list his condo too soon in case it sold before he and Kyle could move upstairs. And Millie. He was really looking forward to the addition of Millie to his household, and, he believed, so was she. When he asked her about how things were going with her nephew and his family, she'd shake her head and ask how soon he thought the penthouse would be ready for them.

Now. Now, was when it was ready. As of today, they could move in. So as not to create any further delays, Ben hired a moving company to pack and move them. As soon as he left to drop Kyle at school, the movers would arrive, begin packing and moving boxes up the freight elevator to the penthouse. Millie would arrive by nine o'clock to direct the move and tell the movers where to place their things. Ben felt comfortable letting Millie make all such decisions. She seemed to care about such things, while he didn't. Besides, she likely knew more about organizing a household than did he. Especially a house with a small child.

The furniture that he, Mel and Kyle had chosen weeks ago was to be delivered right after lunch. By the time Kyle got home from school, everything should be in place.

Millie was a godsend. When Ben was unable to take Kyle to school, she would be able to do it. When Ben could not make it to the school at three thirty to pick up his son, Millie said she would be glad to. As much as he appreciated that offer, he found himself more and more often making an excuse to leave work mid-afternoon to go to the school. He liked going to get Kyle, even going a bit early so he could watch his son in action in the classroom.

He had improved. Ben was astounded at the rate with which Kyle had grown and changed. Already, he was becoming more social. Ben saw him talking to kids, playing with kids and even better, solving problems with them. That was a big part of Mel's room - problem solving. She didn't teach so much as she let them discover. Watching, Ben realized that this did not happen by accident. The activities and the problems were carefully staged, set up so that the students would have to think and to discover and try and work together.

Ben could see the similarities to what he did in his company. Mel was actually training these kids to be future employees, working together, solving problems together. It was amazing to watch and so different from what Ben remembered of school.

For him, much of school was a torturous bore. Endless days of remaining seated in a hard wooden chair, chairs that were made for only one size body - the size Ben never was. School days varied between listening to the incessant drone of a teacher, or doing page after page of monotonous, repetitive, meaningless question after question that had little connection to the real world.

He was not sure he remembered kindergarten. If he did, he could not have been anything exciting like the room that Mel ran. His earliest school memories were of sitting in rows of desks, having knuckles rapped for talking, standing in the corner for not responding fast enough and longing for recess. It's not that Ben didn't like learning - he did. He actually did. It's just that he wanted to learn what he wanted, when he wanted and how he wanted. Those traits certainly did not fit school the way he remembered it.

But things must be different now, or at least they were for Kyle in Mel's room. And, not just for Kyle, but for all the children. From what Ben could gather Mel set up work or explore stations or gave the kids problems, then let them have at it. Some of their attempts at solutions worked out, some didn't. That did not seem to matter to Mel or to the kids. The goal seemed to be to explore and to learn and to work together.

It was almost time to go for Kyle and Ben was bracing himself. The ride up in the elevator was still shaky. Shaky, but getting better. On Mel's instruction, Ben had practiced with Kyle over and over, anticipating moving day when riding the elevator would become a necessity. Kyle was getting more comfortable but it still was not his favorite thing.

From clinging to Ben's neck like a desperate monkey facing imminent death, with practice Kyle had loosened his grip. Slightly. Ben's neck no longer bore the marks of Kyle's nails and his little fingers. Quickly Ben had learned to cut his son's finger nails short enough so they were no longer lethal to his father's jugular. Kyle's little body no longer shook in Ben's arms as they suffered the ride up or down.

They still made the trip in Ben's arms but the little boy's grip was not as much a stranglehold and breathing not as frantic. He seemed to recover a bit sooner after each trip, even opening his eyes at the sound of the elevator door opening. He could now bear to wait as his father placed him on the ground, rather than scrambling down Ben's legs, coming close to unmanning his dad each time.

Yes, even in this, his son was making progress.

A thought struck Ben. It was one thing for him to carry Kyle up and down in the elevator that way, but how could he ever expect Millie to cope? She didn't have Ben's strength and while she might be able to lift Kyle for a couple seconds, she could not bear his weight long enough for the elevator to make it to the top floor. Nor could Ben run the risk that Kyle might hurt Millie in his panic.

It looked like he needed Mel's advice, yet again.

Mel. What would they have done without her? He hated to think of where he and Kyle might have been. He reflected back to those first few days of him and Kyle on their own, their tentative approaches, and their suspicion of each other and lack of understanding. They were strangers, literally and figuratively. While they shared blood, that was it. Neither had laid eyes on the other, ever before.

Now that he had a taste of what it meant to be a parent, Ben could not believe that he'd allowed himself to miss any part at all of his son's life. Certainly he'd not even known of Kyle's existence for his first two years, but once Deanna told him he was a father, nothing should have stood in his way of getting to know this little boy.

In fact, when Deanna first called him, while she spoke on the phone, Ben had been on the computer, booking a flight to Los Angeles. His first instinct had been to fly out immediately to see this new life. But Deanna told him no. She didn't want him to come, saying it would confuse Kyle to suddenly be confronted with two daddies. She was recently living with Neil and didn't want anything to interfere with the budding relationship between her fiancé and her son.

Out of respect for her wishes, Ben had complied and cancelled his flight. He had believed that Deanna, as the mother, knew what was best for their child. It hadn't entered his head that Deanna might not have had Kyle's best interests foremost in her mind.

He still wasn't sure. Really, she'd abandoned their son. Sure, she had brought Kyle to his natural father, but to let him go? The thought was inconceivable. And how many times had she called to check on him in the months since. Twice? Maybe three times? Now that Ben knew Kyle and had a taste of what parenthood was all about he could not imagine his life without Kyle. Ever. If someone tried to take him away he would fight with every fibre of his being to keep Kyle with him.

Yes, life with this child could be difficult and downright frustrating at times. But whose life runs smoothly? Certainly not his. And, the difficult moments were so worth it when the little guy threw his arms around Ben's neck. Or when he settled in beside him for a cuddle as they watched a Dora the Explorer DVD.

Yes, life with Kyle was good.

A gloomy, rainy day, Mel thought as she glanced out of her classroom window. One of those days where the natural light coming in those windows was not enough. She rarely used the overhead fluorescent lights as their barely perceptive flicker bothered some kids who had visual sensitivities. Although more economical to run, if Mel had her way, she'd ban fluorescents from all schools. On sunny days, the windows provided most of the illumination in her classroom. But on days like today the halogen task lights gave a cozy glow scattered throughout the room. Mel and Lori found that the lower light levels had a slight soothing effect on the kids.

Mel's eyes settled on Kyle, bent over the fort he was creating out of wooden blocks. Although he played alongside, rather than with the boy nearby, it was coming. His interactions with other kids were increasing as was his tolerance of their ideas into his games.

Her goal for Kyle today was to keep everything as calm and routine as possible because he was in for a big change after school. Today was moving day for he and Ben.

She went over in her mind the plans she'd helped Ben with so far and how she'd assist after school. She was doing this for Kyle, she told herself. The more settled her students were in their personal lives, the smoother the classroom ran; a win-win for all concerned.

Her conscience gave a twinge. There were ethical boundaries between teachers and students. Although her job often took her in close proximity to the home lives of her kids and she learned more than she might wanted to know about the personal lives of their parents, still there were boundaries.

For a while there, she'd felt that she was going too far over that line and tried to pull back. It was hard though when Ben kept showing up in her room near the end of the school day. Worried, she talked to her principal.

"It started when I ran into them in the park. Kyle was chilled so I invited them back to my place for hot chocolate; I live just down from the park. You should have seen how Kyle opened up to my dog, Max. That was the most verbal I've ever heard him."

"That sounds fairly innocuous," Dr. Hitkins said.

"Well, there's more. Kyle's dad is new to parenting; he's quite clueless in fact, but is trying. His present condo was no place for a child, so he's moving them to a bigger place. Although initially he complained about the furniture in our classroom, he's seen the difference it can make and wanted furnishings suited to Kyle in their new place. He asked my advice on what to get."

"Yes, you'd certainly have some suggestions to offer."

Melanie nodded. She felt guilty not detailing just how involved she had been with her suggestions but couldn't bring herself to talk about their shopping day together. It's a good thing the school year was almost over. In just a few weeks Kyle would be assigned to a new teacher and she would no longer need to feel guilty about her involvement with him. And the rest of his family.

Family. Families were strange things. Melanie thought back to her dinner with hers last Sunday. She cringed recalling her argument with her mother. it was though just a variation of the same fight they'd had over and over and over again.

"No, Jeff didn't have the same chances you had. It's different. You weren't born with autism; he was," her mother said.

"So?" Melanie replied. "So what if he has autism? That's one part of him. What about all the other things that make up Jeff?"

"Melanie, you know he's not strong like you. Life is harder for him. It's my job as his parent to protect him."

"Oh, for...." Melanie blew out a breath. "Look. He has a diagnosis of autism. No one will deny that. But autism does not have to define his life. That's one aspect of it and with it comes challenges and strengths.

"He's smart - smarter than me. Despite having autism, his grade 12 marks were higher than mine and he put in far less effort than I had to. But then life all just stopped for him."

"Well, life is hard for him. He's doing what he likes now. He's fine."

"You call it fine when a thirty-three year old man spends his life in a darkened basement with his face plastered to a computer screen? His only interactions are with made up characters in a computer program."

"No, he spends time with his father and I. He eats one meal a day with us, usually."

"And you think that's enough of a life for my brother? And what's going to happen when you and dad are no longer around?"

They broke off their argument as Jeff came up the stairs.

As they ate the meal their mother had prepared, Melanie had an idea.

"Hey Jeff, I need a favor. Some friends of mine are moving Friday and I'm helping them after school. They're going to be in a big mess and won't feel like cooking supper. Would you make something for us?"

Before he could answer, their mother said, "No. You know how I hate a mess in my kitchen and I need to be getting our own meal ready." Their father kept his eyes on his plate and shoveled the mashed potatoes into his mouth.

As if their mother had never spoken, Jeff said, "How many people?"

"Four adults, counting you and one child."

"No!" from their mother.

"What do they like to eat?"

"I don't think they'll care. But Kyle, the little boy, does not like different foods touching each other."

Jeff grinned. "Well, who does?"

"No. It's out of the question," continued their mother.

"Four, counting me. You want me to eat with you?"

"Yes, definitely," said Mel.

"No, that is going too far. Melanie, I insist you stop taking advantage of your brother right now."

Mel looked at her mother. So far, she'd ignored her. Jeff's ability to hyper-focus worked in his favor in times like this. He'd hardly been aware that their mother was even there. Now both siblings turned to look at her.

"I'm simply asking my brother for his help," Melanie said.

"Well, I think it's unfair of you to even think of asking him to do such a thing. He has his own things to do."

"Like what?" Melanie asked.

"Yeah, like what? Jeff echoed. "I have nothing to do on Friday. Or most other days either."

Their mother raised her other argument. "And just where do you think he's going to do this? You know I hate a mess in my kitchen. I like everything in its place. And these people will hardly have their kitchen ready for Jeff to use."

"He can cook at my place," Mel said.

"And how's he going to get there?"

"Mom, I'm right here. You don't have to talk about me. Mel, I'll take the bus or walk. I'll get there. "

"You still have your key to my place, right?"

"Yeah. I'll call you with the ingredients you'll need to have ready for me. You can add it to the stuff I'll need for the weekend." With that, Jeff left the table and headed for the basement.

"Where are you going, son?" their mother called.

"Gotta plan the menu." And that was the last they saw of Jeff that evening.

"Now look what you've done," her mother chided Melanie. "You've gotten his hopes up and he could get hurt. What if they don't like what he makes? You're expecting him to sit down with strangers and eat? Make small talk during the meal?"

"Yep. It's just a single father named Ben, his housekeeper Millie and his five year old son, Kyle." At Melanie's explanation, her father looked up from his plate.

"Single, you said?" he asked.

Melanie didn't meet his eyes. "Yes. He's new to parenting, just got custody of his son this fall. He's needed some help. Kyle's one of my students. He has autism."

Her mother looked shocked. "He's not going to upset Jeff, is he?"

"Mother!" Melanie tried not to grind her back teeth.

Driving home, Mel regretted fighting yet again with her mother. She reminded herself that most parents do the best they can at the time. But, time worked against her brother. He had not moved on with his life for the past fifteen years, since he finished high school. School had provided a structure to his life and got him out of the house each day. Once that was over, nothing had taken its place. Her parents could not bear the thought of Jeff going out into the world, to further education or to a job. What if people didn't understand him? What if he felt overwhelmed? What if he got scared? What if he didn't know what to do? No, he was safer at home with them where they could look after him.

Partly, her parents went into protection mode because they didn't know what else to do or how to help. It was true that Jeff could become anxious and new situations were difficult for him. Rather than figuring out ways to help him cope or problem solve, their parents hovered and protected, doing everything for their son.

They were not the only ones. An alarmingly small percentage of young adults with high functioning autism and Asperger's Syndrome lived independently. Many suffered from learned helplessness, having been over-helped all their lives. Well, see where this had gotten Jeff so far. Melanie was determined to help Jeff make a better life for himself. And, she was determined that this would not happen to Kyle.

What? Where did that thought come from? Kyle was not her child, not her responsibility. No, but he was her student, at least for a few more weeks. And she strove to help each child in her class to be as independent as possible.

Under Mel's instructions, Ben and Millie went to work. The plan was for Millie to play in the park with Kyle while Mel and Ben got ready for Kyle to come home to the penthouse.

They used the digital camera voraciously. They took pictures of everything imaginable in the new place. Mel kept talking about something called a social story. Ben didn't get it and said that over and over. Mel pretty much told him to just shut up and take the pictures. So, he did.

The pictures were of everything in their new place. He started at the outside door and took pictures of the entrance, the lobby, the elevator button, elevator doors and the open elevator. Then he took a picture of the elevator buttons with a finger pushing P for the penthouse floor. He gave these all to Mel, both printed out and in digital form. She used them to make a social story about Kyle coming home and going in the building. She taped Kyle's name in big block letters beside the P button in the elevator to show him which one to push that first day he was to go in the elevator. Even though Kyle could not reach that high and had to be hoisted up by Ben or Mel, Mel still insisted that Kyle getting to push the button would give him some semblance of control over his environment. He would feel less like things were being done to him and that he had a part in what was happening. If he could feel that he had control and could make things happen, he'd be less fearful.

Next, they took pictures of leaving the elevator and the hallway to the penthouse. Ben took a picture of the door to their new place and a picture of his hand turning the key in the lock.

Then, they were inside. The day before he'd taken pictures of the bathroom and the kitchen and given them to Mel, but not before placing their own towels on the bathroom racks at Mel's insistence. They had to be towels that Kyle used often so he would feel that they were his and that this was not a totally strange place.

Mel made him go back to the store to take pictures of the furniture they'd bought. Ben put his foot down at that and refused unless Mel went with him and Kyle. He'd feel less a fool that way and besides, he just plain enjoyed her company. Any excuse to get her to spend time with them was fine with him. To be honest, it didn't seem to take a lot of arm twisting to get her to come. Maybe, just maybe, she'd had fun, too.

Kyle loved revisiting the furniture store. He remembered what they'd done there last time and raced for a pillow to use to attack his father. he bounced gleefully on the mattress with Mel. While she insisted that they take pictures of the living room furniture and the bed set Ben would use, she spent the most time on the furniture meant especially for Kyle. In the store, she had Ben take detailed photographs of everything that would be in Kyle's room, even though Ben felt like a fool. When they had entered the store, Mel spent a few quiet minutes with the manager and after hearing her explanation, they had not been disturbed.

Mel must have spent the rest of the weekend on her computer, judging by the books she created for his son. What kind of a teacher did that? Didn't teachers spend their evenings marking assignments and grading papers and planning lessons? How did she find the time to do all this work for his son? And, why did she do it?

When he asked her, she said that it was to her benefit to have each of her students as calm and settled as possible because that helped the other kids in the room. Ben had quirked an eyebrow at her. "So, you're telling me that you go to the home of your other students and take pictures, choose furniture and make books for them?" Mel had blushed and mumbled something about that she probably would if asked. Ben just looked at her and she would not meet his gaze.

It gave Ben hope. Maybe as drawn as he felt to Mel, maybe, just maybe she was not reciprocating just for the sake of a poor motherless new student in her class. Yes, she truly did seem to care for Kyle but maybe there was something more as well.

CHAPTER 14

"Are you all set, Jeff?" Mel was in Ben's new penthouse, calling her home number. She had not been one hundred percent sure her brother would pull through and was relieved to hear his voice answer her phone.

"You said you would be here to pick up the food and me at 6:15. It's only 6:07 now. Of course I'm not ready. You won't be here for another seven and a half minutes."

"Okay, okay. You're right. I was just checking. I'm leaving Ben's place now to come get you. I'll be there in five or ten minutes."

"Seven and a half minutes," repeated Jeff.

"Oh," Ben groaned. "Oh, this roast beef sandwich is wonderful. Where'd you find this beef?"

"On the roast," Jeff answered.

"I mean, which deli do you use?"

"I guess you could call it Chez Mel," said Jeff.

"Chez Mel? Our Mel? Have you been holding out on us and you own a deli, Mel?" Ben asked.

"Jeff's referring to my house," explained Mel. "Knowing him, he seasoned and cooked the roast. And, I'd guess he also made the Panini bread. Right, Jeff?" Jeff nodded.

"Is this all you can make?" Ben asked him.

"No, I can make...." Jeff began.

Mel cut him off, knowing that Jeff would give a complete itemized list of every dish he made and that list would go on and on and on. She tried summarizing for Ben the gourmet skills her brother possessed even though he did not have as many opportunities to use them as he'd like.

Ben grew pensive. "Have you worked in a restaurant?" he asked Jeff. Jeff shook his head no.

"Ever thought about it? Ben continued. "I'm thinking more of a deli and bakery rather than a restaurant."

Again, Jeff shook his head.

Mel was her mother's daughter, she realized, and some of her mother's trepidation filled her. What was Ben thinking? Would he suggest something that would be too much for Jeff? Then she sat back. This over-protection was what she accused her mother of. Jeff was a thirty-three year old man. He could make his own decisions.

"My sister runs a bakery. She's run off her feet trying to do everything. She has a couple of kids who help wait tables, but Ellie finds it hard to do all the baking, ordering and managing on her own. And, she's trying to introduce new things in the bakery, things to get more people in there. Food like this sandwich would be ideal."

Jeff listened intently but didn't say anything. Ben waited, getting uncomfortable with the silence.

"Well, if you don't like the idea, that's fine. It was just a thought," Ben said, his eyes not meeting anyone's.

"What idea?" Jeff asked.

Ben stared at him, then looked at Mel. He caught on. "I guess I didn't say what was in my mind. Would you be interested in meeting my sister? In seeing the bakery? Maybe the two of you could talk about the possibility of you helping her out."

Jeff stood up and left the room. No one else moved. He returned a few minutes later with his coat on. "Well," he said, "aren't we going?"

"Going?" Ben asked.

"To meet your sister." Jeff was impatient. "Did you forget what you just said?"

Mel intervened. "Jeff, I don't think Ben meant right now, but some time. Right, Ben?"

"Yeah. What if I call Ellie and set something up for this weekend? Would that work for you?"

Jeff nodded and sat back down to finish his meal.

Life moved on. They settled into the penthouse more or less all right. With Mel's help, they prepared Kyle for the changes. Even though they had showed him the space, he had not seemed to recognize that it had anything to do with them. Telling him did not seem to make it so.

"You talk too much," Mel said.

"What the hell is that supposed to mean?" Ben asked Mel. Attractive as she was, she could really push his buttons.

"When you're frustrated with Kyle, you talk too much. That confuses him even more and gets you more frustrated."

She tried to be patient with Ben and explain. She talked about something she called auditory processing.

See, Kyle could hear all right. Ben knew that for a fact because Deanna had told him she'd had Kyle's hearing checked twice when he was younger. They had thought that perhaps he wasn't talking because of a hearing impairment that made it difficult for him to hear then repeat words.

But no, that was not it. His hearing tested fine both times. And, Ben was sure he could hear all right. He must to be able to have memorized huge dialogues from his Dora videos.

Something must be wrong with Ben's hearing because he had trouble following some of what Mel tried to explain to him. She said that there was a difference between hearing and understanding what was said. Hearing the words was only the very first step. The words had to go into the child's ears, and then the child had to begin to make sense of them. That was where communication often broke down. Then there was yet a third step, where the child had to determine how to respond to what he had heard and understood. This making sense of what he heard was called auditory processing.

And, Kyle's ability to process what he heard varied. Sometimes it was easier than under other circumstances. Take noise for instance. Background noise could make a big difference and his ability to process would go way down. This auditory processing weakness was part of the reason Mel was so big on using visuals – visual schedules, pictures, and pictorial stories. Show, don't tell. Use pictures, not just oral words. And Ben had seen that it did actually make things easier for Kyle.

Mel explained more. For kids with autism spectrum disorders, everything in the environment came at them with the same intensity. For most, especially most adults, our brains automatically filtered out extraneous, background noise. While our senses might register the humming of a fan or the flickering of the fluorescent lights then tune them out, a child with autism would not be able to do such things automatically. If he blocked out all those background noises and concentrated on a voice, it would be through a conscious decision on his part and require concentration. When a skill was not automatic, it required more effort. That is why kids with autism often tire readily. It's taking them so much effort to handle a normal day, far, far more effort than for other typical kids their age.

Ben's heart hurt at the thought of how hard all this was for his son. Mel sharply reprimanded him for any pity he felt.

"Understand it, feel it, but don't pity," she said. "This is the hand the child has been dealt. He knows no different. It's your job as Kyle's father and my job as his teacher to help, to train him and guide him towards independence."

Mel was adamant that there would be no "poor me" or "poor Kyle" under her watch. No siree. Sure, Kyle had challenges, but he also had strengths. They would build on those and teach Kyle how to use his strengths to prop up his challenges and find other ways to do the things that were difficult for him. Isn't that what everyone did?

Yes, Mel had no sympathy for him, Ben. Ben often felt that she was hard on him. She did not cut him any slack, or at least only rarely. Ben had the feeling she was teaching and training him just as much as she was training and teaching and guiding his son. To be honest, though, he needed it. He'd been like a babe in the woods when he first met this kid and again, being honest, without Mel's guidance, he and Kyle would not be where they were today - a team.

Ben's thoughts turned to Mel, as they often did. In fact, it did not seem to take much to make him think of Mel. She had become an integral part of their lives.

Take the move, for instance. Without Mel's instruction, Ben did not think he would have ever gotten Kyle into the elevator. Mind you it was still not smooth, but it was better.

Some of what Mel suggested he didn't get.

"This seems excessive – pretty much useless. Besides, who has time for all this?" Ben asked her.

"Well, you're welcome to try it your way then," Mel retorted.

When he did, usually the result was not what he'd hoped and sometimes it was actually a disaster. He now avoided disasters whenever possible because not only were they hard on him and his ego, but they were hard on Kyle. It was not fair to his son when he did not heed Mel's advice.

How did she seem to know his son so well when she'd met him only a couple days after Ben did?

Sunday afternoon, Ben and Kyle picked up Melanie and Jeff at Mel's house. They drove to the bakery.

As they entered the door, they were met by the tantalizing smells of warm yeast breads. Kyle stopped and went up on his toes, his nose in the air, sniffing with a smile of pleasure on his face. Ellie came from behind the counter, wiping her hands on a towel. She bent down and held out her arms to Kyle. "Come here, Munchkin."

As soon as he spied her, Kyle began a headlong run for his aunt, but at her words stopped short and looked behind him. Nope, no other kid was there. He looked back at Aunt Ellie. She was still crouched, arms outstretched toward him. He checked again behind him, then asked, "Who's Munchkin?"

"You are," Ellie told him.

"I'm Kyle."

"But I'm going to call you Munchkin."

"Why?" he wanted to know.

"Just come here anyway," his aunt told him.

After giving Kyle a hug and a cream puff, Ellie turned to Ben and Mel. "You usually don't bring girls home, big brother. In fact, the last time was like hmmm, well never. What's the occasion?"

"Can it, brat, or I won't introduce you," Ben told her.

"Mel, this is my little sister, Ellie. El, this is Melanie Nicols, Kyle's teacher. We came so that you could meet her brother."

As the women shook hands and chatted a few minutes. Ellie glanced all around, not seeing the brother. Then she spied a strange man fiddling with things behind her counter. "Hey," she yelled. "Get away from there. You're not allowed behind the counter."

The man ignored her. Then they all heard the whoosh of the latte machine steaming milk.

"That thing hasn't worked for weeks! What are you doing back there? How'd you make it do that?" Ellie asked.

"Oh no," said Mel. "Don't ask how. Just accept that he fixed it."

"What?" Ellie didn't get this.

Jeff grinned. "Afraid I'll give too much information, sis?"

"Exactly," Mel agreed. "Don't ask him how he fixed it unless you want the full - and I mean full - explanation. Ellie, I'd like to introduce my brother, Jeff Nicols. Jeff, this is Ben's sister Ellie and the owner of this bakery."

Ellie nodded, but her attention was more on her coffee machine. "Do you think we can actually use it now?"

"If you want a coffee," Jeff told her.

"How the hell did you do that? We worked at it, and had the repair guy out twice. He said it was toast."

"I see why he couldn't fix it," said Jeff. "Anyone who would confuse a coffee maker with a piece of toast does not know what he's doing."

Ellie stared at Jeff. Ben thought this a good time to display what was in the cooler he carried. "Hungry, El?" he asked his sister. Let's have a seat and try the food Jeff made for us.

They joined Kyle and his cream puff while Ben brought out the array of deli sandwiches Jeff had created. They were cut into small slices, made for sampling.

"Oh, this is so luscious," Ellie told Jeff. "I thought I was up on most of the delis and bistros in town but I've never had anything like this. Who do you work for?"

Ben told her that Jeff was not working in any restaurant right now. Melanie shot him a look. He gave her a look back. What he said was technically true.

"Between jobs, eh?" Ellie asked. Without waiting for a response, she rushed on, "Any chance you'd consider working here? Don't worry - no long term commitment if that scares you off. But, we really could use food like this here; our clientele would go for it big time. We'll take any amount of your time you can give us. We can even offer lattes again now, thanks to you. How about it? Interested in helping out here? I can't pay you a lot but we could work something out."

"El, if you'd shut up a minute, Jeff might be able to give you an answer," Ben told her.

"What would I have to do," Jeff asked.

"Make sandwiches like these. Make coffee. Help with the baking. Anything you feel like doing around here."

"Okay."

"Pardon?" Ellie asked.

"Okay. I'll work here," Jeff said.

"That's it? It was that easy? Don't you need to think about it?" Ellie wanted to make sure.

"I already did." Jeff said.

"Did what?"

Jeff looked at Ellie strangely. "Think about it. I already did think about it. Yes, I'll work here."

Although Mel had hoped for something like this, she now had second thoughts. "Wait a minute. What's mom going to say?"

Ellie looked confused. "Your mother? Is that why you're not working right now, because you have to look after her?"

"Not exactly," Mel explained.

"Then, I don't get it. What does your mother have to do with you working here?" She asked Jeff.

"I don't know what she has to do with it," said Jeff.

"Nothing," agreed Mel.

"Nothing," echoed Kyle.

CHAPTER 15

"All right, class. What's our lining up routine?" Ms. Nicols asked.

"One table at a time."

"Arm's length from the person in front of you."

"Hands down at your side."

"Arms crossed over your chest," offered various students.

"Very good. But I'm confused. How do I cross my arms over my chest and put my hands down at my side at the same time?" Melanie hoped for the right answer.

"That's a choice," explained Jordan. "Put your hands at your side or across your chest."

"Excellent." They really did get it, thought Melanie. It had been a good year and now was time to help her students move on to the next teacher.

"There are two grade one classrooms in this school. You will be with some of your friends from this class and you will be making some new friends next year.

"Right now, those who will be in Mr. Johnson's grade one room will come with me for a tour. When I say your name, please line up." She called out the names of about half her class and they headed down the hallway.

"This is Mr. Johnson. He'll be your teacher for grade one next fall," Ms. Nicols told the boys and girls. She pulled out a digital camera and took a picture of Mr. Johnson standing in the doorway waving hello to his future students, then a few of the classroom. These would be added to the booklet each child would receive before summer vacation. Some children like Kyle, who found transitions difficult would have a number of introductory sessions like this one.

When Ben showed up after school for Kyle, Mel took the two of them to meet Mr. Johnson. She took pictures of the cubby where Kyle would hang his coat, the desk where he would sit, the inside and outside of the washroom he'd use and where the schedule was kept on the wall. While Mr. Johnson chatted with Ben, he encouraged Kyle to explore the room, check out the view from his desk and generally get a feel for the room. Kyle would have the chance to do this several times this month to help prepare him for next fall.

"Isn't this overkill?" Ben asked when Melanie presented him with Kyle's book of pictures.

"In my experience, it helps. But, suit yourself," Melanie replied. Ben sighed.

That night as he tucked Kyle into bed, Ben opened up Kyle's Grade One book. While he read the captions, Kyle studied each picture. Even though Melanie had suggested they go through this every night, Ben was sure Kyle'd have it memorized within a couple days.

"Good man," Ben told his son several weeks later.

"Good man," echoed Kyle, his voice small and tentative.

Ben settled his hands more firmly on Kyle's shoulders. Although it was still far from perfect, Kyle's comfort level with riding the elevator increased daily. He'd graduated from enduring the ride with his limbs plastered around his father's torso and his face buried in Ben's neck to now standing on his own feet. To feel secure he needed to be pressed firmly into an adult, with pressure on his shoulders. His little body tensed but no longer trembled during the ride. Together, he and Ben counted off the floor numbers as each lit up. Ben faithfully followed Mel's instructions to practice the elevator ride so that Kyle would be able to do it with Millie. Once again, her advice worked.

"Someday champ, you'll be taking this ride all on your own," Ben told his son.

With Millie around, Ben was able to get more work done in the evenings. As Mel had predicted, Kyle liked to sit at his own little desk while Ben worked. Tonight he was looking over his Grade One book. He brought it over to Ben and squeezed between the desk and chair until he could perch on his dad's lap. Kyle pointed to the book. Ben stifled his impatience at the interruption; this was important to Kyle and the work could wait. Still, he thought....

Bye now, Kyle repeated the words with Ben.

"This is Mr. Johnson, Kyle's teacher. This is where Kyle will hang his coat. This is Kyle's desk..." and so on until Ben thought they had covered every possible aspect of a grade one child's life. But, day after day, Kyle stared intently at each photograph.

As Ben lifted Kyle down from his knee, he thought the little boy felt heavier. "I think you've grown, Kyle. You're getting to be quite the little man, getting bigger every day. Soon you'll be doing so many more things on your own. I'm so proud of my big boy Kyle."

Kyle wandered out of the room. Soon Ben could hear one of the endless Dora DVDs playing. He'd long since gotten over his nervousness at Kyle using his equipment. The kid could probably teach him a few things about the components. Millie was in the kitchen preparing dinner.

A while later, the meal was ready and Millie called them to the kitchen. Ben went to wash his hands and called for Kyle to do the same. When Kyle didn't appear in the bathroom, Ben assumed his son had gone to use the kitchen sink.

When Ben entered the kitchen, Millie asked, "Where's Kyle?"

"I thought he was in here with you. He must be engrossed in his DVD. I'll go get him."

Millie said, "No, you sit down and I'll go fetch him."

She returned a minute later with a frown. "He's not in the living room or in his bedroom."

"He must have dozed off somewhere. Let's take a look."

It didn't take long for them to scour the whole place, looking in most spots twice. There were only so many spots for a little boy to hide. Ben called out to his son but there was no reply. He yelled louder, hoping to wake Kyle up if he'd fallen asleep. The silence was deafening. Ben's and Millie's steps got faster as their voices raised. On his way to check the hall closet yet again, Ben noticed that the condo's door to the outside hallway was ajar. He was positive he'd shut it when he came home.

With a sinking feeling, Ben opened the door and peered into hall, hoping to spy his son. No such luck. With his heart in his throat, Ben checked the hooks beside the door, the ones he'd put at the just right height for a small boy to hang his coat. Empty. Kyle's jacket was missing.

He wouldn't. He couldn't. Kyle would not leave the condo. Why would he? There was no place to go in the hallway. It was small with only two doors - the one to their condo and the one for the elevator. Kyle hated the elevator, so he certainly would not go there. But, he had been getting better at riding it. No, he would not do that, he'd never wander off on his own.

Is that what all parents of lost children said, Ben wondered? No. Kyle was not lost. He had just fallen asleep someplace in the condo. You know how deeply children can sleep. He'd not heard them calling; that was it. That had to be it.

Ben returned to the condo, and with Millie's help searched every last inch of the place again. No Kyle.

"Millie, will you stay here, please? I'll check the elevator just in case Kyle did go in there. He could be huddled in the corner, scared to death. He was too small to push the button for the penthouse, so he wouldn't be able to get back home."

Ben had a long wait for the elevator, indicating that it must have been on the ground floor. He rode down, trying to talk himself calm. No Kyle.

The doorman was snoozing behind the counter. Ben's voice woke him. "Have you seen a little boy go by here by himself? This would have been in the last half hour or so," Ben told him.

"No, I haven't seen anyone come in or out in the last while and definitely not a kid alone."

"My son. I thought he was in the living room but when we called him for supper there was no answer. We live in the penthouse and can't find him anywhere. He's only five."

"Did you check the stairwell?"

Damn. How could Ben have forgotten about that? There were three doors in his hallway, not just two. He'd never taken the stairs since they moved to the penthouse, but Kyle had been used to the stairs when they lived on the third floor.

"Thanks. I'll go up that way and check."

"All fifteen floors?" the doorman's question was spoken to thin air as Ben dashed for the stairwell.

Ben paused on the seventh floor landing. How could he have let himself get this out of shape? He took a few deep breaths and continued up three more floors. He paused there to use his cell phone to call Millie. Maybe she'd found Kyle.

"Millie, any luck?" Ben asked.

"No. I was hoping you were calling to say you found him."

"The doorman hasn't seen anyone go out for the past half hour but asked if I'd tried the stairwell." Ben huffed as he plodded up. "I'm four floors down from you now. Maybe we'll find him on the landing of our floor. See you in a minute."

Ben had only made it up one more floor when his cell rang. "You found him?" he asked.

"No, but the doorman called. He checked the videotapes. I didn't know but the elevator is on video camera. He can see Kyle. He wants us to come down to his desk."

Ben opened the door to the nearest hallway and pressed the elevator button. When it came, Millie was already in it. Together they counted the seconds until the car landed in the lobby.

The doorman was ready for them with a freeze frame on the monitor. "There. See?" he pointed. There, in grainy black and white was Kyle, alone in the elevator. He pushed the L button for lobby and rode down, his arms rigidly at his sides, concentration on his face. When the doors on the lobby, Kyle hesitated as if he was going to leave the car, then went back in. They watched as he jumped and jumped, trying to hit the P at the top of the panel, the button that would send the elevator car back up to Kyle's home. Try as he could, Kyle was too short.

Next, he put his backpack on the ground. Ben grimaced. He had not even noticed that it was gone. Some father he was. Kyle stood on his back pack, trying to gain some height. Still not enough. Kyle sat in the corner, with his knees drawn up under his chin. He clutched the back pack to him. Ben's heart broke watching his son. When a tear slid down Kyle's cheek, Millie grabbed Ben's arm and her own tears began.

Ben put his arm around Millie as they watched. Kyle stood and pressed the button to open the elevator door. The last the video showed of him was one little boy leaving the elevator.

"Where'd he go? Where's the rest of the video?" Ben demanded.

"That's all there is," explained the doorman. There's only a camera in the elevator, then one outside the front door."

"Can you pull that one up?"

"Just give me a minute."

"We don't have a minute! My son could be out there. He's only five and he's alone and it's getting dark and he has autism and he hardly talks! He'll be scared out of his mind and anything could happen to him. I need that video now!"

"Ben," Millie patted his arm. "It's here."

They could see Kyle on the screen now, his dark jacket fading in with the growing shadows outside. It took him several tries but he finally got the outer door opened and went through. He hesitated just an instant then turned left down the street.

Ben snarled at the other man. "I thought you said no one went in or out for the past half hour?"

"Honest. I didn't see anyone enter or leave. I do remember the door making some noise but I thought it was the wind blowing it. You know how it's been gusting. Besides I was sitting behind the counter. I can certainly see any adult coming or going but your little boy's head would have been below counter height, so I would have missed him."

Ben wanted to turn on him. He needed to take this out on someone. But the important thing right now was Kyle.

"Call 9-1-1 will you?" Ben said to the doorman. "When he has them on the line, would you give them a description, Millie?"

"Yes. Are you calling Mel?"

"You bet."

Both the cruiser and Mel pulled up at about the same time, both parking diagonally and part on the sidewalk.

While Millie returned to the penthouse to get the officers copies of Kyle's school pictures and Kyle's Grade One book, Ben tried to think of where Kyle might have headed. Nothing came to mind.

197

"We sometimes go to the park off that way. Yes, that's the direction Kyle went, but it's almost dark. He never wants to play with other kids there, just with me."

"He doesn't play with other kids? Who are his friends and where do they live?"

Melanie stepped in. "Kyle's friends are mainly the kids in his class but he only sees them during school time. Right, Ben? He doesn't play with them other than at school, right?" Ben nodded.

Melanie explained that Kyle had autism. She told them that when they called, he might not respond to his name. Sirens and flashing lights might spook him, making him feel the need to hide from strangers looking for him.

"But would he come if you call?" they asked Ben.

Ben hesitated. What kind of a father did this make him?

Again, Melanie helped. "People with autism are sensitive to sound, lights and touch. What might not bother you at all could seem like fingernails on a blackboard to someone like Kyle. It's hard to predict how he will react in an unusual situation. He's not used to being out at night alone."

Ben's panic was rising. "Why are we standing around here yakking? My son's out there somewhere. He's alone. He could be cold and scared. What if some creep picks him up? Shit, he's only five. He doesn't know about all the weirdoes in the world. So far he's only met people who help him. We need to get our asses in the saddle and find him!"

"Mr. Wickens, as we speak there are two patrol cars and four officers at his school. They're scouring the ground looking for him. There's a call in to the school principal to meet us there to unlock the doors just in case he found a way to get in. They'll turn on all the lights in the school and the principal and an officer will stay there just in case Kyle makes his way there.

"Two other officers are in the park checking for him. They've just started their sweep. Now, if you could tell us where else you think he might have gone...."

A policeman came up to them. "Your housekeeper said you wouldn't mind if we used your scanner and computer. Your son's picture has now gone out to all our officers. While I did that, Millie ran off copies of his photo on your printer. We'll sweep the blocks surrounding your place then hand out pictures at any businesses that are open."

He continued. "Now, we need someone to stay in your apartment in case Kyle returns on his own. Your housekeeper volunteered. The doorman will stay on alert here and notify us if he sees your son. Do you two want to stay here and wait? If you're up to it, given that this kid has autism, it might help if you would check the park as well. Maybe he'll come to you even if he won't respond to an officer. Do you have cell phones on you?"

Ben and Mel nodded and gave him their numbers. "Wait right here while I patch your numbers through to dispatch so we can call you right away if we see him."

Mel wrapped her arms around Ben. It was hard to tell if she was giving or receiving comfort, but it didn't really matter anyway. She was the one thing Ben could hang on to in the middle of this whole mess.

They were given the go-ahead and started for the park, calling Kyle's name as they went. They entered the park and passed the swings and slide. They passed the spot where Ben and Kyle had made piles of leaves and jumped through them. They passed the bench when Melanie had waited and they threw leaves on her head. Everywhere they went, they called Kyle's name but there was no response.

They came to the other end of the park, Ben's despair growing. He turned to retrace his steps, but Mel was rooted to the spot, looking off down the street.

"He wouldn't," she said. "No, it's too far and he wouldn't remember the way."

"What way? What are you talking about?"

"Ben, you don't think he'd walk all the way to my place, do you? Remember that day in the park? He had such a good time, and then afterwards you came to my place for hot chocolate. Kyle played with Max."

"Shit, he's only five years old. He's only been to your place a few times and the last time we drove, not walked. That's a long ways for a small kid alone and in the dark."

"He had fun at my place. He probably felt safe and secure there."

"I have no better ideas, so we might as well go look." Ben checked his cell just in case there was a message and he for some reason hadn't heard it ring. No such luck.

They continued in silence for a block, holding hands.

"First thing tomorrow morning, I'm calling Deanna. No. As soon as we find Kyle I'm calling her. She can come and get him in the morning, "Ben said.

Melanie stopped walking to search Ben's face in the light from the street lamp. "But, why? Why would you want to give him up?"

"Why? WHY? Because I'm a goddamned unfit father, that's why. Because I can't look after my own kid. I can't keep him safe. Look at all the things that have happened to him since I've had him. He almost dies in a fire. He cracks his bloody head open. And now, I can't even keep track of one little kid and here he's lost in the dark all alone." Ben's voice cracked.

Melanie just held him. There was nothing she could say right now that would help him see all the good things that had happened to Kyle this past year.

"Come, on. Let's go check out your place. I can't figure out what else to do." Ben's shoulder's stooped. His head was down. As he berated himself in his mind, he momentarily forgot to scour the bushes they passed but Melanie watched for him.

As they approached Melanie's house, Ben could see that her lights were off. For some reason, he had hoped to see all her lights blazing with Kyle cozily ensconced in her living room. But, how could he be? She would have locked her doors when she left, of course.

Melanie stopped as they entered the front gate. "That's funny," she said. "Usually Max hears me coming down the street and by the time I get to the yard he's here waiting to greet me."

"Did you leave him locked in the house?"

"No. I definitely remember leaving him outside. Let's go around the back way and see what's going on."

As they walked around the side of the house, flashes of Kyle and Max tearing around the yard came to Ben's mind. He'd have to get the kid a dog. Kyle really enjoyed Max and dogs were good protection. It would have to be a big dog, one like Max.

Melanie grabbed Ben's arm. "Shhh," she said and pointed. There on the chaise lounge was Max, his head in the air pointed towards them, his tail thumping on the chair pad. His body was curled around a small shape. Although Max's tail continued to wag, his head went back down and he would not meet Mel's eyes. "He knows he's now allowed on the chairs," she explained.

But she'd forgive him this time. For in between his big paws was the head of one little boy. As they hustled up, they could see Kyle's chest rising and falling, one arm draped over the big German Shepherd.

"God," was all Ben could say. He fell to his knees beside the sleeping boy and placed one hand on his son's tousled hair and the other on the dog's shoulder. Steak every day. Caviar. Anything this dog wanted, it was his. He had stayed and protected his son. Kyle was safe. He was safe.

Safe! Holy shit. The city was full of policeman out looking for his son. He turned to hear a low voice. Mel was on her cell, letting the police department know that they'd found Kyle. She clicked off and dialed another number. Now there were tears in her voice as she told Millie that Kyle was fine and where he was. They'd be bringing him home soon.

Meanwhile, Ben nudged Max out of the way and picked up his son in his arms. He just stood there holding him, his head bowed and his eyes closed. Melanie rested her head on Ben's other shoulder and held them both close.

Kyle stirred. His half-awake gaze rested on his father's face. "Max and me had a sleep," he told Ben.

"I can see that, bud. We'll have you back home in bed in no time. Just rest. I've got you."

CHAPTER 16

"Ben, come back to bed. Kyle's all right now." Mel was dressed in Ben's bath robe. Through the glow of the night light in Kyle's room, she could see the deeply sleeping little boy. Ben sat on a child-sized bean bag chair, his chin on his fists, staring at his son.

He looked up at where Mel stood, silhouetted in the doorway. "I take that back about calling Deanna. I'm a selfish bastard, but I can't imagine my life without him. God, I can't believe how close I came to losing him."

"But you didn't. He's not the first kid to ever wander off. Lots of parents get scares like this. We'll just have to teach Kyle more, show him more rules and work on what to do if he gets lost."

Ben looked over his hands at Mel. "We?" he asked.

It was too dark for Ben to see her blush. "Sorry. I meant you. I guess I was thinking that I'm his teacher and we could do more of this at school. But I'm not his teacher anymore, so my official involvement is over."

"It doesn't have to be."

"What do you mean?"

"I mean that you can have as much involvement in Kyle's life as you want. And in my life. We need you. I need you."

Melanie didn't know what to say. But, as always, she was direct. "What are you saying?"

Ben rose and came towards her, pulling Kyle's door partially closed. "I mean I need you and want you. I think I've been showing you that for months now. I may have used Kyle as an excuse to get you close but it was not just for Kyle's sake that I kept calling you. And tonight, in my room, didn't I show you how I felt about you?

"I love you, Melanie Nicols. I want to be with you; I want you to be with Kyle and I. Would you marry us? I'll take you anyway I can have you. If I'm going too fast and you don't want to get married, you could live here with us or we could get another place. Or you could stay at your place and we could take this a little slower if you need to."

"I thought accountants were cautious, careful planners, not the impulsive types."

"This isn't impulsive. I've thought about it for a long time now, just wasn't sure how to bring it up. Well, actually, my first goal was to get you in my bed, but now I want longer term." He peered down at her, trying to make out her expression in the darkened hallway.

Melanie took his hand and pulled him back toward his bedroom.

"Wait," Ben said. "Don't I get an answer? Even an 'I'll need to think about it'?"

"Yes, if you want a formal answer. Now, get in here. This calls for more action than for talk."

Millie made waffles while Mel turned the bacon. Kyle seemed none the worse for his adventure. Melanie and Ben glowed as they teased one another and touched often. Millie was the quiet one of the bunch.

It took a while for Ben to notice Millie's withdrawn mood, but finally Mel's pointed looks made him pay attention.

"Millie, are you feeling all right?" he asked. "Is anything wrong?"

"No, I'm fine. I wondered if I might have the rest of the day off. I have some things to do and would like to visit my nephew. I presume Mel will be sticking around? She'll help with Kyle, I'm sure."

"Sure, I can stay," Mel assured her, a question in her voice. "Is there something you'd planned for supper that you'd like me to make?"

"No. I'm sure you have your own ideas," she said as she left the room.

Melanie and Ben looked at each other. This was not like Millie.

"Just let me get my keys and I'll give you a ride," Ben called.

The first half of the ride to Millie's house was silent. Millie stared out the window. Ben did not know what to say. Well, obviously guessing was not going to work, so he'd better just ask her. But ask what, he wondered.

Millie spoke first. "So, it looks like you and Melanie are an item."

"I'm not sure I would have put it that way, but yes, we are together. Definitely together now." He grinned at Millie. "Last night she agreed to marry me. Marry us - Kyle and me."

Millie smiled back at him, but her enthusiasm didn't reach her eyes. "Congratulations. I'm very happy for all of you. She'll make a lovely mother to Kyle. She's a wonderful young woman."

Ben felt the but coming.

And, it did. "But I guess this changes things. Kyle will have a mother now to look after him. You won't need a housekeeper."

Ben looked at her then laughed. "I'm not marrying Mel to get a housekeeper. Nothing's changed that way. We still need you. In fact probably more than ever. Who will stay with Kyle this summer if you're not there?"

"Well, teachers don't work in the summer. Mel will be home with Kyle."

"Some teachers don't work in summer, but not Mel. Ever heard of extended school year? Mel begins next week teaching at the middle years school; she'll be there four days a week all summer."

Millie had more worries. "Some women like to be mistress of their own home. They don't want another female mucking around their place."

"Does that sound like Mel to you? You can ask her yourself, but as far as I can see, she thinks it's a real boon that Kyle and I come with a housekeeper. And, she likes you, she really does."

"I'd better talk directly to her about this. I don't want to interfere or stay where I'm not wanted."

Ben thought a minute. "There is a problem. We can't stay where we are. I can hardly stand the thought of keeping Kyle in that condo another minute after what we went through last night. A condo is no place for a child. We have to get a house, a house with a back yard where we can have Max."

They pulled into Millie's driveway. They sat and took in the views of the house.

"God, you have a lovely place, Millie. A fenced yard, the verandas, the dormers, and look at this neighborhood. It's a place where families live."

"I love it, but I'm aware of all the repairs it needs. Once my nephew and his family leave I hope to get started on some of them. If I keep renting the place out, I should be able to afford to fix up a few things now and then. Really, I should sell it but I have such good memories of the place that I hate the thought of strangers living here."

Ben looked at her. "When does your nephew leave again?"

"In just a few weeks now."

"And how many bedrooms did you say are in this place?"

"Five."

There was a pause. "Mel's accused me of being impulsive. That's a strange thing to say to an accountant. And to think my life was so orderly this time last year." Ben took a big breath. "Millie, would you consider selling to me? Then we could all live here together, you, Kyle, Mel and me. Or, if you don't want to sell, we could rent from you. Either way, we could work something out."

Millie said nothing. Then, Ben remembered. "Of course, I'd have to check it out with Mel first. I think she'll like the idea, in fact I bet she'll be excited. We were talking last night about how we need to find another place to rent or buy, a place with room for Kyle and Max."

Still, Millie was silent. Then a tear trickled down her cheek. Shit, thought Ben. Why didn't I keep my big mouth shut? And, where's Mel when I need her? Looks like I have to do this on my own.

"Okay, Millie. Bad idea, I guess. Sorry. Just forget it. We'll work something else out. It's just that your house really appeals to me - has since the first time I saw it."

"No. Don't forget it. I'm just overcome. I've missed my house. To think of living back here with you and the little one and Melanie and maybe more little ones to come."

Ben had not really thought about that last part, but yes, a smile spread across his face. He could see it. "Let's go talk to Mel. Oh, but wait. Do you need to think about it some more?"

"My head's too full to think of details right now. I imagine there's a lot to work out."

"We get the place appraised to find the fair market value. That would tell us the price either way, if I was to buy it from you or just rent. And we could get a lawyer to work out the details about how you'd always have a place here, even if I bought it."

"Bless you. But we're getting a little ahead of ourselves. Go on home and see what that bride-to-be of yours thinks of your impulsive offer."

Mel, it turns out, was ecstatic, especially after she toured the place. Kyle didn't really get what all the excitement was about, but when Ben said, "Where shall we go to celebrate?" Kyle had an answer.

"To the bakery! Yeah!"

The smells of strong coffee and yeasty dough greeted Millie, Mel, Ben and Kyle when they entered the bakery. Kyle yelled, "Munchkin's here!" It was a good thing his yell warned Ellie before he launched himself at her. Jeff waved a hand at them, but didn't turn his attention from the mocha latte he was building.

Ellie settled them at a table to take their orders. "Why don't you have Jeff waiting tables?" Ben asked her.

"I found that his talents really lie behind the counter. He might be a whiz at cooking, but customer service isn't exactly his forte." She and Melanie exchanged a grin. "Business has picked up since he's been here. We're in the black and it looks like we'll stay there. His sandwiches are a big hit."

"That's great news, little sister." Ben gave her a hug. "We have some news of our own."

"Well, give," Ellie said.

"Ms. Nicols lives with us only I don't have to call her Ms. Nicols, only if I want to. I can call her Mel or I can call her Mom, too."

Ellie's eyes rose. She looked questioningly from Ben to Mel.

"Yes, that's true," said Mel."

The door to the bakery opened and in walked Mel's and Jeff's parents. Since Jeff had started work there they had become regular patrons. At first they came to hover and worry but gradually they'd relaxed as they saw their son blossom. He was a competent, contributing member of the bakery team.

The door from the kitchen opened and Ben and Ellie's parents came out. Ben raised his eyebrows at Ellie. "Yeah dad dropped in, but mom has been coming with him lately, keeping him in check and they don't stay long. Everything's good," she assured him. "And now we're in for one big family adventure. Time to spill your news, big brother."

"Adventure?" asked Kyle. He began singing, "Dora, the explorer..."

ITEMS MENTIONED IN SCHOOL DAZE

Williams, Mary Sue and Shellenberger, Sherry. *How Does Your Engine Run?* ®, *A Leader's Guide to The Alert Program for Self-Regulation*. Therapy Works, Inc., 2009.
http://www.AlertProgram.com

Hokki™ (http://www.vs-furniture.com/761.0.html?&L=1&FL=10).

Peanut ball chair
(http://www.therapyshoppe.com/therapy/index.php?main_page=index&cPath=3&products_id=2086&sort=20a&page=1).

Seating disc
(http://www.therapyshoppe.com/therapy/index.php?main_page=index&cPath=3&products_id=1781&sort=20a&page=1).

Ball with feet
(http://www.therapyshoppe.com/therapy/index.php?main_page=index&cPath=3&products_id=2090&sort=20a&page=1).

Time Magazine named Temple Grandin one of the one hundred most influential people of our times.
(http://www.time.com/time/specials/packages/article/0,28804,1984685_1984949_1985222,00.html).

Theraband™
(http://www.google.ca/search?q=theraband&hl=en&qscrl=1&nord=1&rlz=1T4GGLL_enCA330US332&biw=1270&bih=555&prmd=imvns&tbm=isch&tbo=u&source=univ&sa=X&ei=fE-GT5T1HIauiQL558T6Dw&sqi=2&ved=0CJIBELAE)

ENJOYED THIS BOOK?

If you enjoyed the book, please leave a review on Amazon (http://www.amazon.com/Autism-Goes-School-Book-Series-ebook/dp/B0085HN9HQ) or the online store where you may have purchased this book.

Join us for books 2 through 5 in the series:

Autism Runs Away
Autism Belongs
Autism Talks & Talks
Autism Grows Up
Autism Boxed Set (contains Autism Goes to School, Autism Runs Away and Autism Belongs
Autism Goes to School Workbook (coming in 2017)
Prequel to Autism Goes to School (coming in 2017)

Come back and see how Kyle, Ben, Mel and their friends are doing, and meet more students of Madson School. You'll find them on Amazon at: https://www.amazon.com/Dr.-Sharon-A.-Mitchell/e/B008MPJCYA

Turn the page for a synopsis of the other books in the series.

OTHER BOOKS IN THE SERIES

Autism Runs Away

Ethan is only in grade one and already has been *kicked out of one school* due to his tantrums and pattern of running away when in a panic. Now, his mom's enrolled him in a new school but remains glued to her phone, waiting for the call to tell her to come pick him up, that they can't handle him, that they don't know what to do with a child who has autism.

How can she trust these strangers to look after her son, just one small child among hundreds, when he has run from own parents so very many times? They don't know the terror of losing your child in a mall or watching him run blindly into traffic.

What started as a fun chase game when Ethan was a toddler has turned into a terrifying deviation. The adults in his life never know when he might take off.

Rather than attaching an adult to his side to keep him safe, this new teacher talks about calming strategies and choices. Do they not realize what could happen if Ethan flees the building? The impact of a car on one small body? Sara is about to learn if this new school is up to the challenge.

Meet Kyle, Mel, Ben and the other characters you got to know in the Amazon bestseller Autism Goes to School. See what they've been up to in the last year and how they join forces to help Ethan.

Go to this link for free sample chapters in all formats:
http://dl.bookfunnel.com/aht0bv1bsg

You'll find Autism Runs Away on Amazon at
https://www.amazon.com/Autism-Runs-Away-Book-School-ebook/dp/B01FCYQ7DC

Autism Belongs

Manny is not like other children. He doesn't talk. He doesn't leave the house. His parents desperately try to arrange their world so that Manny does not get upset. Because, when he does, well, the aggression was getting worse. Too many times Tomas had to leave work to rescue his wife from the havoc of their son's meltdowns. At ten, Manny was becoming difficult to handle.

Passing by a bakery made all the difference. There, they met people who understand autism, along with its strengths and challenges. They learn ways to help Manny communicate and socialize and to have his needs met.

Dare they consider letting him go to school? Is there a chance that Manny actually belongs there? You bet

Meet Kyle, Ben, Mel and the other characters you read about in the Amazon bestseller *Autism Goes to School* and see how they've grown and progressed.

For free sample chapters (in all formats), head to http://dl.bookfunnel.com/5ayjfgrfa4.

You can find Autism Belongs on Amazon at this URL: https://www.amazon.com/Autism-Belongs-School-Daze-Book-ebook/dp/B0184ZQMI6/.

Autism Talks and Talks

Karen is a grade 6 student who has Asperger's Syndrome. She is bright, vivacious and highly verbal. Too verbal. She finds certain topics fascinating, studies them in-depth and is all too willing to share her knowledge with others. She goes on and on and on, not realizing that she is boring and alienating the other kids with her endless monologues. Her protective mom tries to shield her from the world, limiting her contact with peers in case she might be bullied.

Karen would like to be social. She remains on the fringe, looking at other adolescents having fun together and wondering if she could ever be a part of the group.

Karen has potential. Her inability to read body language and her lack of knowledge in social pragmatics get in the way of interacting with others her age and having friends. Through a structured group at school, she begins to understand the give and take of conversation and to have some positive experiences with her peers.

And, can a young man with Asperger's find love?

For free sample chapters (in all formats), head to http://dl.bookfunnel.com/43chbwntbp.

Autism Talks and Talks is on Amazon at https://www.amazon.com/Autism-Talks-Book-School-Daze-ebook/dp/B01IIUZH3S

Autism Grows Up

At twenty-one, Suzie has withdrawn from a world she finds alien and confusing. Ability is not the problem, nor is interest – many things fascinate her. But, she has Asperger's Syndrome and high anxiety. To her, the world is a harsh, scary place where she does not fit.

Suzie lives with her mother, Amanda. She spends much of her day sleeping and most of her nights on the computer. Her mom wishes Suzie would get a job, go to school or at least help out around the house. Suzie feels that her time is amply filled with the compelling world lurking within her comp.

Amanda has two full time jobs – one involves working at the office every day, the second involves looking after Suzie. Amanda wants more for Suze, but does not know how to help her move forward. When she tries putting pressure on her, Suzie suffers from paralyzing anxiety, resulting in morose withdrawal or worse, lengthy tantrums. Suzie is most content when alone in the basement with her computer. Staring at her monitor, the rest of the world falls away and she feels at home.

Amanda is torn. She met this gentleman, Jack. It would be nice to spend time with someone other than her brother and daughter but Suzie wouldn't like it and she needs her mother desperately. Amanda's brother asks uncomfortable questions like what will become of Suzie if something happens to Amanda.

Jack gently persists and Amanda glimpses what her life could be like. Suzie resents the time her mom spends with Jack and makes her mother pay for the hours not devoted to her daughter.

When, they have a home invasion Amanda has only Suzie to rely on.

For free sample chapters in all formats, head to this link: http://dl.bookfunnel.com/x4inimkeym

Autism Grows Up is for sale on Amazon at https://www.amazon.com/Autism-Grows-School-Daze-Book-ebook/dp/B01JB8QW3U.

Autism Goes to School Workbook

Readers who followed Ben and Kyle's journey in Autism Goes to School have said that they would like a guide to help them follow the strategies that Ben and Kyle try. Of course, not every strategy works for everyone. Remember that once you've met a child with autism, you have met one child with autism. While we're all unique, there is often a core cluster of characteristics that kids on the spectrum share.

The workbook looks at the things Ben did right and the mistakes he made, despite his good intentions. It looks at Kyle's responses, then guides you to consider how your child with autism might respond.

There is space to profile your son, daughter or student's strengths and the areas that pose the most challenge right now.

The guide will help you look at the sensory issues that might contribute to the difficulties and ways to help. It discusses the communicative aspect of behavior and how you can help the child better express his wants and needs in appropriate ways. A self-regulated child is a calmer, happier child.

There are examples of visuals and schedules and space to create your own. And, there is an extensive list of references that will help you guide your child to be as independent as he can be.

The Autism Goes to School Workbook will be available on Amazon in 2017.

Prequel to Autism Goes to School

Readers have asked about the lives of Jeff and Mel prior to Autism Goes to School. Coming in 2017 you can read their stories. Go along with Jeff to his first try at college and living away from home. Follow Mel's path as she learns more autism spectrum disorders. Learn about the struggles as their family struggles with the balance of protecting Jeff and fostering his independence.

This Prequel will be out in 2017.

And, of course, you can get your FREE copy of Autism Goes to School in all formats here: http://dl.bookfunnel.com/wpj2sanl3g.

WHAT PEOPLE SAY ABOUT
SHARON'S WRITING AND PRESENTATIONS:

Wow. I have chills. You have answered my questions in ways that many doctors, professionals and teachers could not.

Sharon's advice is on the mark! I have researched and read everything I could get my hands on...and she gave me more useful information than any I've come across so far. She has given me new hope and best of all an action plan to work with for my son.

Wow, you gave me so much great information that I have never heard about from anyone before.

Thank you so much! This was the best advice I have received from anyone. I feel that I now know what direction to go in. Extremely helpful and very informative. Detailed information and support given. Excellent... highly recommended.

Ms. Mitchell... provided me with so much relief! Thank you for giving me some peace of mind and for responding so quickly!

I was literally crying from the stress before this... Thanks.

Your response was also very sensitive and acknowledged my feelings about the situation... Thank you!

ABOUT THE AUTHOR

Dr. Sharon A. Mitchell has a Ph.D. in Psychology Management, specializing in autism spectrum disorders. Her Master's work looked at the long-term outlook for young people with Asperger's Syndrome and high functioning autism. Her career has been spent as a consultant, counselor and special education teacher. Her passion is helping young people, particularly those with autism, to become as independent as possible.

She is also co-author of the Amazon bestseller The Official Autism 101 Manual. To read more about her autism work, visit:

http://www.drsharonmitchell.org

Interested in being part of the **Review Team**? **Review Team** members receive free, Advanced Reader Copies of new books, participate in, developing characters and plots. Sign up at http://www.drsharonmitchell.org.

Dr. Mitchell loves connecting with readers. Please email her at questions@drsharonmitchell.org with comments, ideas or suggestions for future books or to be alerted when the next books come out.

Made in the USA
San Bernardino, CA
16 June 2017